Sophie Calle

Introduction by Clément Chéroux

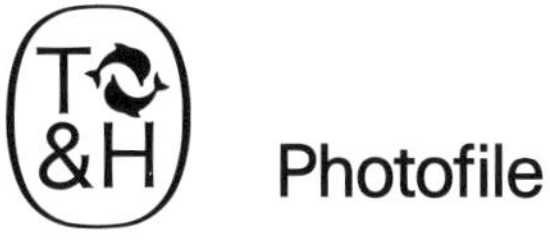

Photofile

Either... or ... and at the same time

The double bind. As a birthday present, a father gives his daughter
two pairs of sunglasses, one white and the other red. When he next
sees her, noticing that she is wearing the white pair, he says to her:
"I knew that you didn't like the red ones!" Another time, when she
has the red ones on, he asks her: "Don't you like the white ones?"
On a subsequent occasion, when she appears wearing *both pairs* of
sunglasses on her nose, he exclaims: "My child, you're mad!" This
story could easily be one of those that Sophie Calle so loves to
tell. Apart from a few key details, which have been altered for the
purposes of this introduction (in the original version, it is a mother
who presents her son with two ties in different colors), this is in
fact a famous textbook case used in psychology to describe the
double bind. In a context of human relationships with authority
(family, work, religion, army, state, etc.), this notion, also called
a *contradictory injunction* or *paradoxical loop*, indicates a situation of
communication in which the messages are at the same time linked,
contrary and incompatible. The double bind obliges to obey while
disobeying. Initially proposed as a theory to explain the development
of schizophrenia, the double bind can be the cause of doubts and
malaise. The French Wikipedia page on the double bind is illustrated
by a photograph of a road sign indicating a dead end, to which has
been added an additional sign reading "except cemetery".[1] That image
could also appear in a book or an exhibition by Sophie Calle. It would
certainly not seem out of place since the artist's entire body of work is
infused with this culture of paradox. Right from the beginning, in the
late 1970s, she never stopped drawing comparisons between reality
and imagination, automatism and control, presence and absence,
hiding and revealing, playfulness and death. This introduction is built
around these fertile oppositions, in the belief that they are absolutely
crucial to the richness, the openness and, perhaps above all, the power
of attraction of the work of Sophie Calle.

Reality/Imagination. Publishing a book entitled *True Stories*, which nevertheless contains multiple invented elements. Asking people who were born blind to describe their image of beauty. Using real small ads as the catalyst for as many fictions. Remaining at the top of the Eiffel Tower, from seven in the evening until seven the following morning, listening to strangers telling stories like Scheherazade in order to keep her awake. Spending a different night in the Saint-Arnoult tollbooth on the A10 motorway, asking motorists to answer questions about travel. It is no secret to anyone that Sophie Calle loves *stories*: those that she tells as much as those that she hears. In the previous generation, the *nouveau roman* ("new novel") had shunned traditional narrative for its excessive use of romance, intrigue and anecdote. Nothing could be worse for the author of the *nouveau roman* than to be blessed—in the words of Alain Robbe-Grillet, the master of the *nouveau roman*—with "a great talent for storytelling".[2] Sophie Calle has intentionally revived the pleasure of these little stories that we whisper into each other's ears at nightfall. As shown in the photograph of her *Sleepless Night* at the Eiffel Tower in 2002, which depicts her body in an upright position, her eyes open and her head resting on a pillow, she particularly likes tall tales. Her stories are often so surprising that they are difficult to believe. The artist also says that for years, her interviewers were mostly content to ask whether her stories were true. It was for this reason that she produced the book with the programmatic title *True Stories*, first published in French in 1994. But it is not enough to claim that one is telling the truth to be believed and journalists continued to ask her if her *true* stories were *really* true. With the popularization of fictionalized autobiography in literature, the booming number of reality TV shows and the growth of social media, the public started to become more aware that just because someone is talking about themselves, this does not necessarily mean they are telling the truth. The discourse of the intimate is an imaginary construction to varying degrees, like all other forms of representation. The question of true or false is not definitively the key issue. It is what the story evokes or provokes that matters.

Automatism/Control. Trailing a man at random through the streets
of Paris and later allowing herself to follow in his footsteps as far
as Venice. Asking her mother to hire a private detective from the
Duluc agency to shadow her. Eating food of a single color on any
given day for six days. Appropriating the surveillance images from
an ATM. Setting off to find her future on the beaches of the Channel
coast, following the instructions of a clairvoyant. Living out aspects
of a storyline devised by the American writer Paul Auster in one
of his novels. Sophie Calle likes automatism. She invents rules,
subjects herself to prearranged procedures, sometimes quite rigid,
and which are often transformed into rituals. She reveres, above all,
chance encounters, amazing coincidences, and what, in the wake of
Guillaume Apollinaire and the Surrealists, is described as a "poetics of
surprise". She creates situations with no purpose other than to favour
the burgeoning of these blossoms of chance: something unexpected
can thus occur. It would be tempting to think that the artist seeks in
this way to abandon herself entirely to chance, as though she wished
for things to escape her control, or for chance to make her decisions.
But, in her everyday life, she readily admits that she is a "control
freak".[3] In an interview with the newspaper *Le Monde*, she recounted
that as a teenager, during the course of an alcohol-fuelled evening,
she fell into a drunken stupor.[4] The next day she remembered
nothing, but no one wanted to speak to her anymore. She then
promised herself that she would never allow this to happen again.
"If I realize that I am about to lose control, I disappear," she explains.
S.C., Sophie Calle's initials, could therefore just as well stand for 'sans
contrôle' (out of control) as 'sous contrôle' (under control). Art, unlike
life, is perhaps indeed the place in which she finds herself escaping
from this obsession about control. In her works, she decides the rules
of the game. She is free to choose whether to obey—or not.

Presence/Absence. Adding her own belongings to those that
Sigmund Freud carefully kept in the study of his final home in
London. Photographing mattresses, lots of mattresses, and also some
beds. Filling fifteen glass-fronted cabinets with presents that were

given to her at birthday parties at which the number of guests exactly matched her age in years. Displaying the image of a red telephone, a wedding dress or a white terrycloth bathrobe. Assembling a collection of stuffed animals in her home. The works of Sophie Calle are teeming with objects. But their nature as objects—their shape, their function, their design—is not, however, what principally interests her. They are instead traces of an experience, of a relationship and, more often than not, the evocation of a person. The bird's-eye view of her childhood bed, which she had slept in until the age of seventeen, abandoned in the courtyard of a Parisian building (the bed had been placed in a room that her mother let out and the tenant set himself alight on it). The birthday gifts represent all her invited guests. The bathrobe is the lover that she never saw naked, at her request, from the front. The fox, the beaver, the ram and the flamingos: each of the stuffed animals that haunt her apartment corresponds to someone dear to her. "When I meet someone new," she explains, "I immediately look for who they might resemble, and I try to find an animal that matches. When my mother died, I bought a giraffe, because she looked down at me from above, with sadness and irony."[5] It is these objects' power of incarnation that interests her. While, to most observers, they appear *inanimate*, they are to her undeniably endowed with a soul, that is to say, *animated*, in a sense close to the word's etymology. Sophie Calle *objectifies* her nearest and dearest at the same time as she *subjectifies* her objects. But perhaps the most astonishing thing is that, when looking at them, we never really know if they are the metaphor of a presence or an absence.

Hiding/Revealing. Calling the contacts in an address book to ask for information about its owner, then publishing her findings in the *Libération* newspaper. Getting a job as a maid in a Venetian hotel, examining the personal belongings of the rooms' occupants and photographing them. Reading her mother's private diary in public. Opening her bed to strangers. Posing almost entirely naked at a striptease joint in the Pigalle district of Paris. For years, Sophie Calle has endeavoured to reveal, through her works, what is generally considered to be intimate. With a certain love of risk, the artist has

striven to reveal lives as much as she has exposed herself. She has
practised, at a highly sophisticated level, the art of indiscretion,
with the aim of highlighting how apparently ordinary lives can
sometimes contain the extraordinary. Then, from a particular
moment onward, and it would be interesting to know what it
corresponds to in her personal thought processes, she turned the
principle of confidentiality inside out like a glove. She, in her turn,
became the custodian of others' secrets. In a graveyard at Saint-
Servais in the Côtes-d'Armor, in the Cemetery of Kings (Plainpalais
Cemetery) in Geneva, in Green-Wood Cemetery in Brooklyn
and at Château La Coste in the parish of Puy-Sainte-Réparade in
Provence, Sophie Calle acquired plots and invited the living from
the surrounding area to come and bury their own secrets. Another
work, from 2014, entitled in fact *Secrets*, consisted of two identical
safe-deposit boxes containing a couple's respective secrets. Safe-
deposit boxes, coffins, tombstones, as well as tollbooths and phone
booths: in Sophie Calle's work, secrets often assume the shape of
rectangular boxes. The first time she exhibited *Suite vénitienne*, it was
in a confessional. Visitors sat in the priest's place and, in a long,
muffled whisper, the penitents delivered their stories. Nowadays, it
is she who acts as confidante. She no longer reveals secrets. She has
become silent as the grave.

Playfulness/Death. Photographing tombstones in American
cemeteries that feature the generic designations "Father", "Mother",
"Sister", "Brother", etc., in place of family names. Arranging the
funeral of a cat named Souris (meaning "Mouse"). Endlessly writing
and rewriting her will. Envisaging her burial as a final performance.
Filming her mother during the last months of her life in an attempt
to capture the very moment of death, without success. Like many
of us, Sophie Calle is haunted by death, but with the difference
that she makes it the very medium of her art. The blog of La
Chambre Syndicale Nationale de l'Art Funéraire, a trade association
representing the funeral industry, hits the nail on the head when, in
addition to providing advice on burying loved ones, selecting a coffin
and choosing between burial and cremation, it devotes an article to

the artist entitled "Death lies at the heart of Sophie Calle's work".[6] And when it is not death that obsesses her, it is sleep or absence, which are its metaphorical forms. Nor should we be surprised at the magnetic attraction she feels toward blind people. "Les aveugles" ("The Blind"), "La dernière image" ("The Last Image"), "La couleur aveugle' ("Blind Color"): several series bear witness to this. For an artist whose life is so intimately connected to sight, it seems quite logical that issues surrounding the loss of sight should become a recurring theme. Nevertheless, despite the unmistakable presence of death, the work of Sophie Calle is rarely morbid. Perhaps this is because she constantly compensates for the gravity of her subjects with a deliberately light approach. She has, she says, "a taste for things that are sad", which she tries "to experience lightly".[7] Her "coming to terms with the dead", to borrow the title of a film by Pascale Ferran, is negotiated in the form of a game. When asked if she is a player, she readily replies that she likes to organize playful rituals.[8] By re-enacting, in a quirky fashion, the funerary rites of modern Western society—the will, the plot, the tomb, the burial, the service—not only does she de-dramatize them, but she also shows how absurd they can sometimes be. It is her way of warding off death.

The supreme point. Psychology, communication and systems theory, as developed from the 1950s onward in the United States by the Palo Alto Group, showed that there were several ways to attenuate the grip of the double bind. Dialogue—in other words, the opportunity for the two protagonists to reflect together on what put them in such a situation—is one of them. Humour is another way to reduce the pressure generated by its grip, and art constitutes a third form of accommodation. Even though the notion of the double bind was not formulated until the mid-twentieth century, it has been a favoured mechanism of art since antiquity. The Gordian knot, the paradox of Buridan's ass or the Cornelian dilemma: there are indeed many texts which, from Greek tragedy to street theatre, use its narrative or dramatic resources. Closer to home, Surrealism also played a part in this. In his *Second Manifesto of Surrealism*, first published in the December 1929 issue of *La Révolution surréaliste*, André Breton wrote:

"Everything leads us to believe that there exists a certain point in the mind where life and death, the real and the imaginary, the past and the future, the communicable and the incommunicable, the high and the low, cease to be perceived as contradictory. One seeks in vain any other motive in Surrealist activity than the hope of finding that point."[9] Although in 1953, the year in which Sophie Calle was born, André Breton wrote a final manifesto, *Du surréalisme en ses œuvres vives*, seemingly a desire to continue the flame of the movement, it was already faltering. Sophie Calle has therefore never been part of Surrealism, but she keeps alive some of its most brilliant sparks: the love of surprise, play and paradox, to mention but a few. She pursues the quest for that 'supreme point' in which double binds—reality and imagination, automatism and control, presence and absence, hiding and revealing, playfulness and death—are no longer perceived as opposites.

Clément Chéroux

Notes

1 See: fr.wikipedia.org/wiki/Double_contrainte (accessed October 13, 2021).

2 Alain Robbe-Grillet, 'Un joli talent de conteur…', *France Observateur*, no. 390, 31 October 1957, p. 19.

3 Clément Chéroux, 'Sophie Calle, je ne vous aime plus depuis que tout le monde vous aime', *La Voix du voir. Les grands entretiens de la Fondation Henri Cartier-Bresson*, Paris: Fondation Henri Cartier-Bresson/Xavier Barral, 2019, p. 240.

4 Laurent Carpentier, 'Sophie Calle, ma mémoire, ce sont les photos', *Le Monde*, 14 August 2021, at: www.lemonde.fr/series-d-ete/article/2021/08/14/sophie-calle-ma-memoire-ce-sont-les-photos_6091411_3451060.html (accessed October 13, 2021)

5 Clément Chéroux, 'Sophie Calle, je ne vous aime plus depuis que tout le monde vous aime', *art. cit.*, p. 248.

6 See: deces-info.fr/blog/mort-centre-loeuvre-sophie-calle (accessed October 13, 2021)

7 Fabian Stech, 'Sophie Calle – Je déteste les interviews!' [2002], in *J'ai parlé avec Lavier, Annette Messager, Sylvie Fleury, Hirschhorn, Pierre Huyghe, Delvoye, D. G.-F., Hou Hanru, Sophie Calle, Ming, Sans et Bourriaud*, Dijon: Les Presses du réel, 2007, pp. 92–93.

8 Clément Chéroux, 'Sophie Calle, je ne vous aime plus depuis que tout le monde vous aime', p. 234.

9 André Breton, *Second manifeste du surréalisme* [1930], in *Oeuvres complètes*, Paris: Gallimard, 1988, vol. I, p. 809.

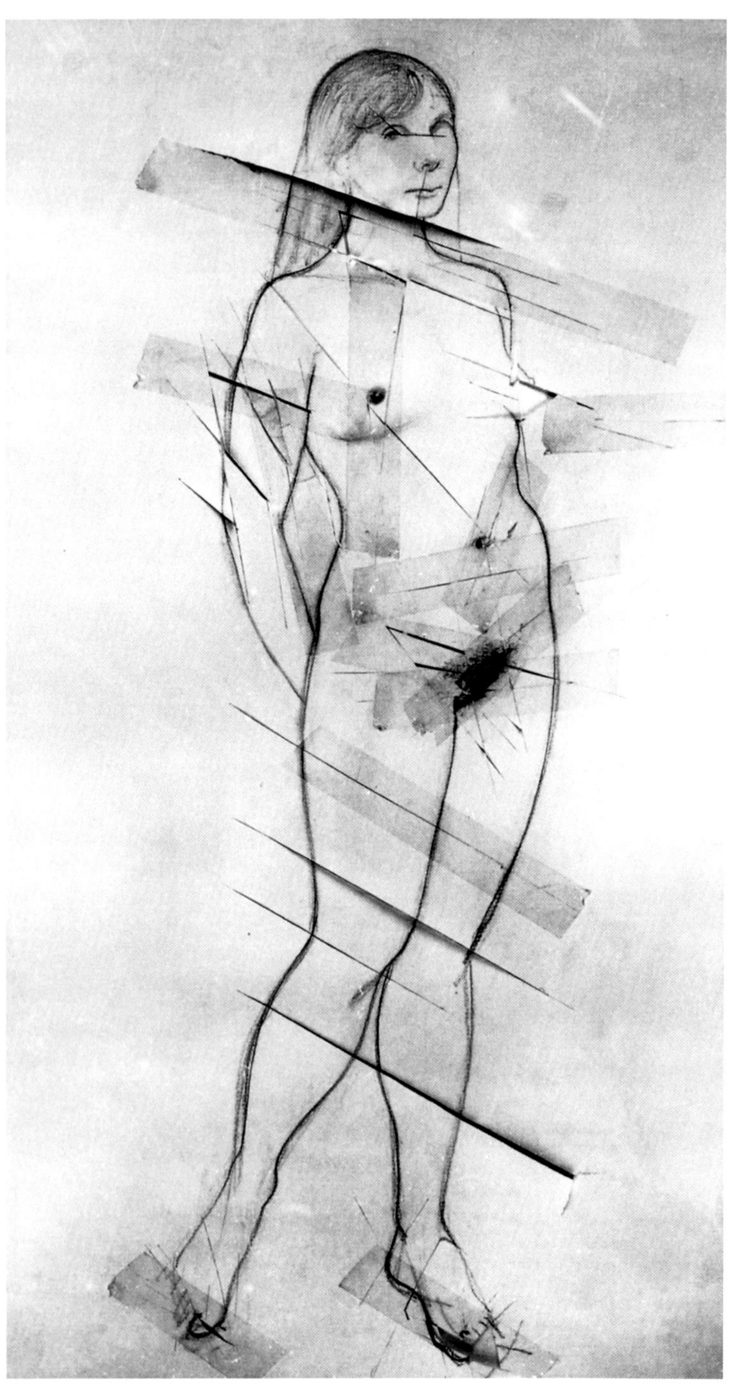

True Stories

Autobiographies, 1998–2020...

Wait For Me

I was two. It happened on a beach—Deauville, I think. My mother had
entrusted me to a group of children. I was the youngest and they had
to get rid of me: that was their game. They huddled together, whispering,
then burst out laughing and scattered when I tried to come near.
And I ran after them, shouting: "Wait for me! Wait for me!"
I can still remember.

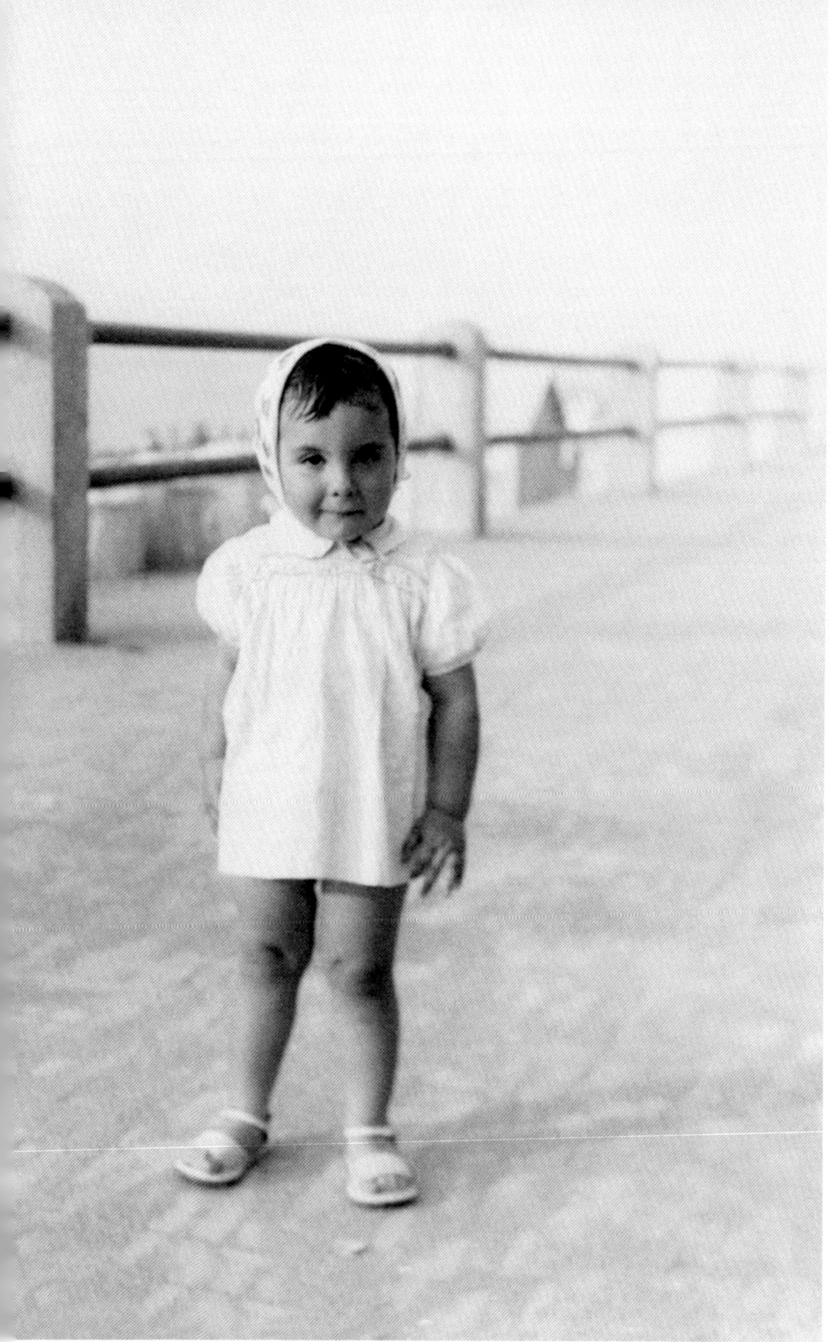

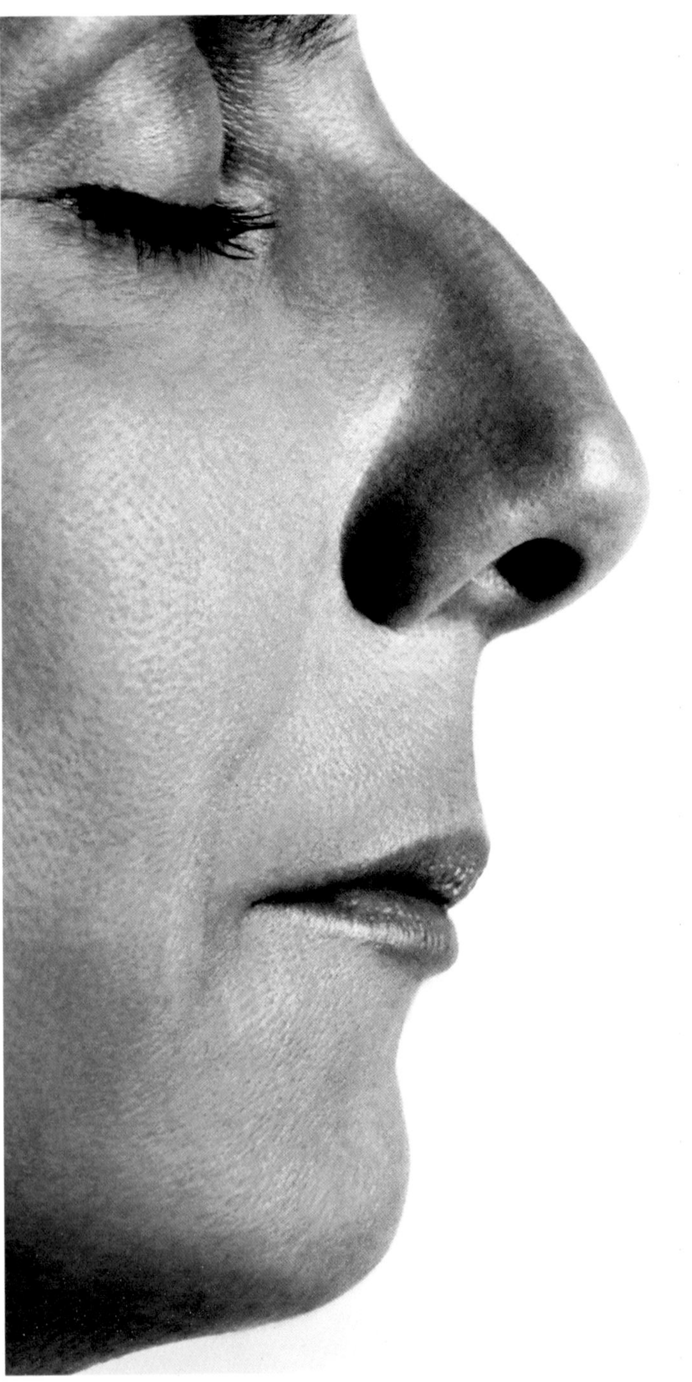

The Plastic Surgery

When I was fourteen my grandparents suggested that I needed plastic surgery. They made an appointment with a famous cosmetic surgeon, and it was decided that my nose should be straightened, that a scar on my left leg should be covered up with a piece of skin taken from my ass and that my ears should be pulled back. I had doubts, but they reassured me, I could change my mind up until the very last moment. In the end, though, it was Doctor F. himself who put an end to my dilemma. Two days before the operation, he committed suicide.

The Pig

It's a silly story. I was about thirty. A man phoned to say that he and I were making similar work and that we should meet. I always worry I might miss out on something so I agreed. When he arrived he told me his art consisted of stopping women in the street and asking them to sleep with him. Well, he said, wasn't one of my projects all about getting strangers to spend time in my bed? He told me he was taking me to a barbecue. I spent the whole evening playing the maid, grilling sausages, serving and cleaning up. Time goes by faster when you're busy. Later he dropped me off outside my door. He leaned in to me and sought my lips. I pushed him away. "What makes you think I'd want to kiss you?" I protested. "Well anyway," he answered, "you eat like a pig." Even today, after all these years, his words haunt me. I can't remember a thing about him, yet he's still sitting at my table.

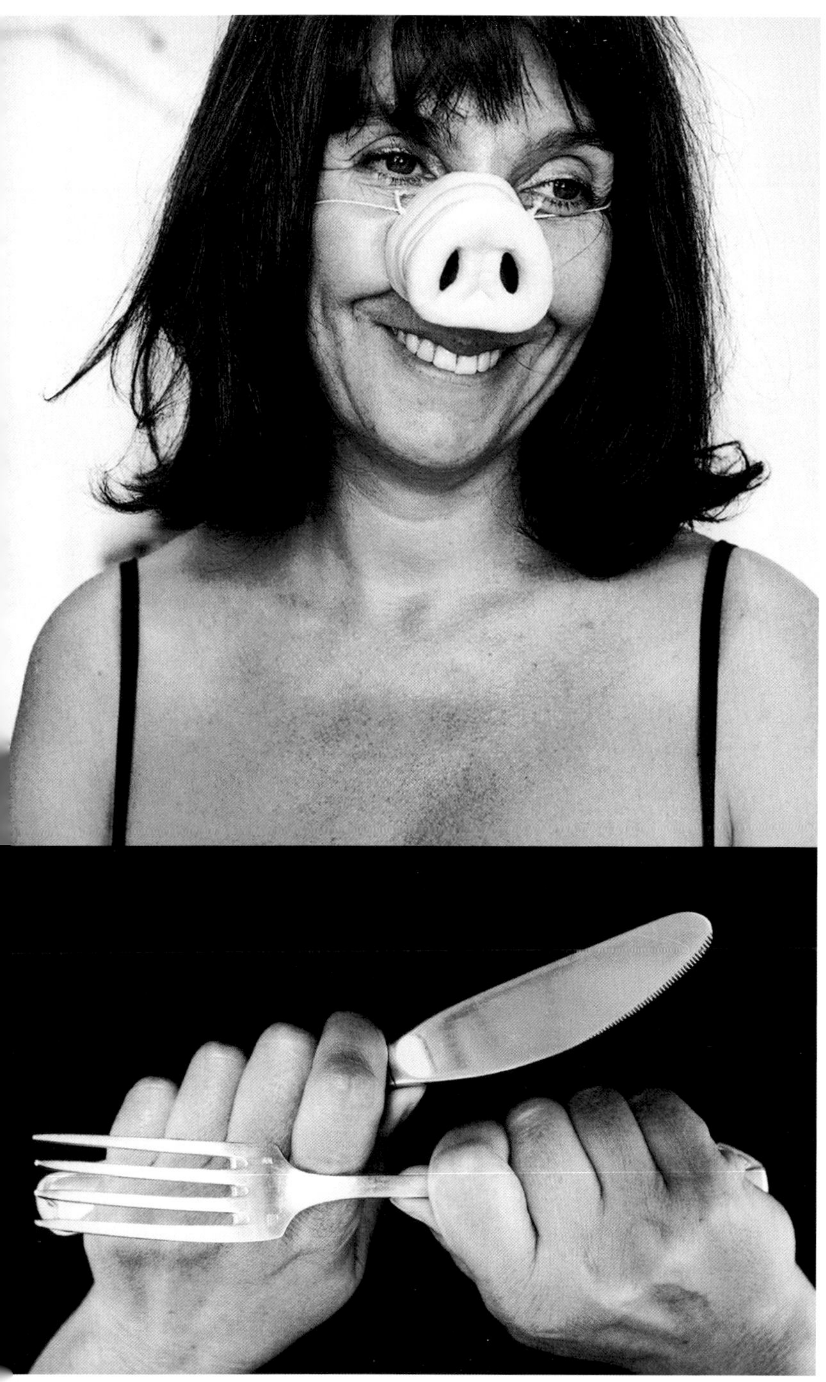

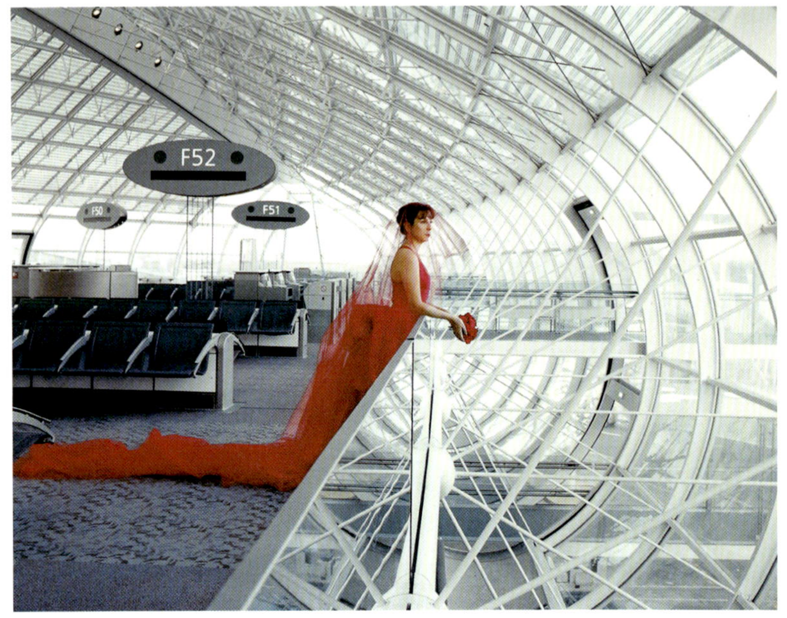

Dream Wedding

I nearly got married to a man who had been posted to China for three years. That's a long time. Like a fiancée whose betrothed is bound for the front, I wanted to marry him on the runway at Roissy airport, just before he left. The groom would step up into the plane as I stood on the tarmac. The reception would be held without him and I would spend my wedding night alone. We set the date for October 7, 2000. Negotiations with the airport authorities, mayor's agreement to officiate, license, guest list, dress—everything was ready. Until a letter from the state prosecutor arrived refusing permission. Weddings had to be celebrated on municipal premises, with two exceptions: hospital, in the likelihood of imminent death of one of the betrothed, or prison. So, town hall, jail, agony, these were our choices. Banal, radical or tragic. Still, on October 7, I did go to the airport to wear my dress, just once, and to grieve for our wedding. And I did go back home alone, as planned.

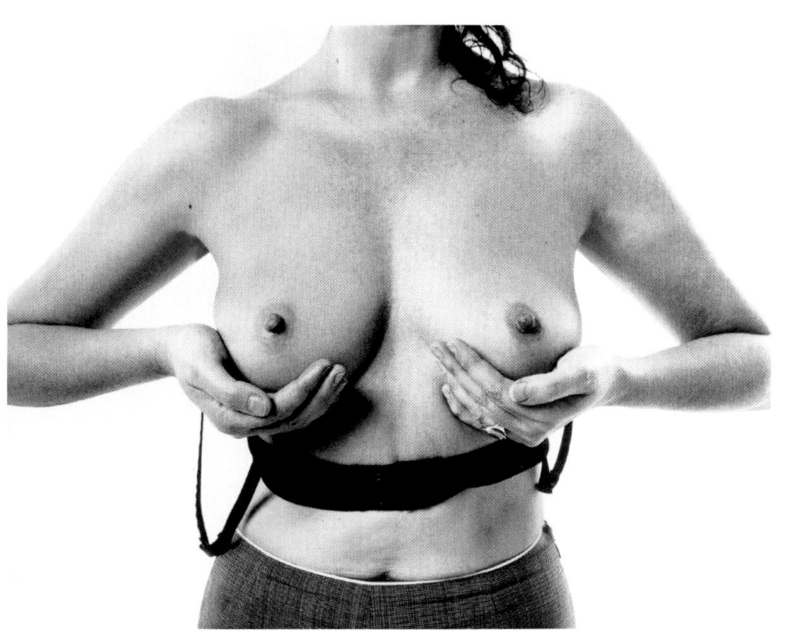

The Breasts

I was a flat-chested teenager. Still, wanting to be like my friends, I bought a bra, a *soutien-gorge* which, of course, I didn't need. My mother, who possessed a magnificent bosom and a sharp wit, called it my "*soutien-rien*"—my support-nothing. I can still hear her words today. Over the years that followed my chest slowly pushed out. Nothing to write home about, though. Suddenly, in 1992, a transformation occurred. In the space of six months, spontaneously, I had proper tits: no treatments, no operations. A miracle. I swear. I was thrilled, but not really surprised. I put this feat down to twenty years of frustration, envy, dreams and sighs.

You really fooled them!

I once had a show at the Museum of Modern Art in New York. My mother came to the opening. When she discovered my works hanging among those of Hopper and Magritte, she was amazed. With no malice whatsoever, she cried out: "You really fooled them!"

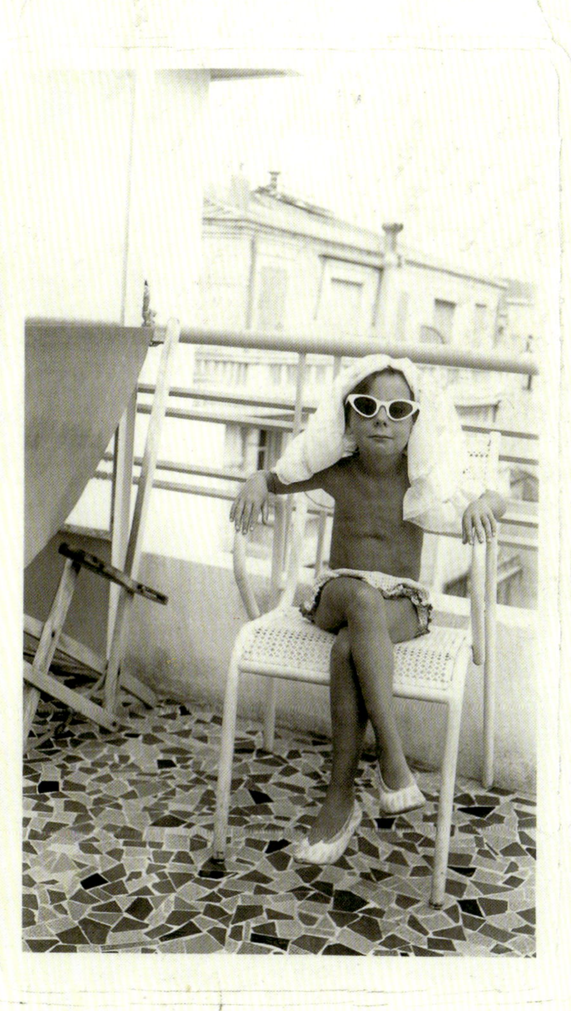

"And you, expecting something special?"

To Victor Hasselblad

I never wanted children. Imagine a sad day: I'm feeling lonely and dreading nightfall. Here comes a young couple, the man with his arm around the woman's waist, the woman pushing a stroller. Their eyes tell me to give way: An offspring bestows certain rights. They gaze blissfully at the baby. And I sigh: "Poor things …" Not a reasonable reaction, I know, but I feel better already.

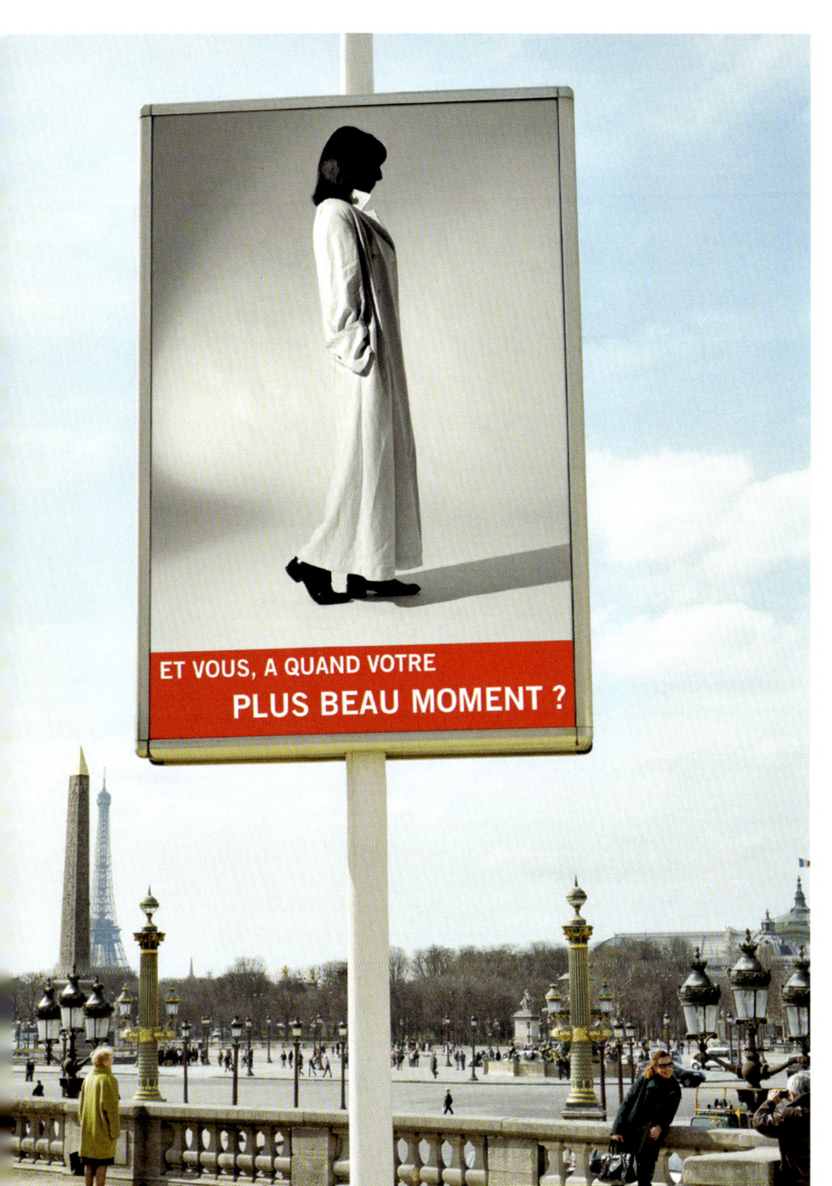

ET VOUS, A QUAND VOTRE
PLUS BEAU MOMENT ?

Motherhood

I never wanted to have children. But, as I was insisting upon this, someone pointed out that I behaved toward Souris as though I were his mother. It was true; I was enchanted by his grace. He was the funniest, the smartest; his portrait was my screen saver. Whenever, as they always do, parents showed pictures of their children I, never to be outdone, pulled out one of him. And so I decided to take the next step and give birth to my cat. I asked my vet for advice in order to simulate a pregnancy for the usual gestation period (58 to 63 days) and purchased a small black and white stuffed toy. I never went through with it. Was it because summer was the wrong time to be wearing a fake belly? Or, because I feared being made fun of by my friends in the village? In the winter, I was traveling, hanging shows ... As I kept postponing motherhood, Souris grew old. It no longer made any sense.

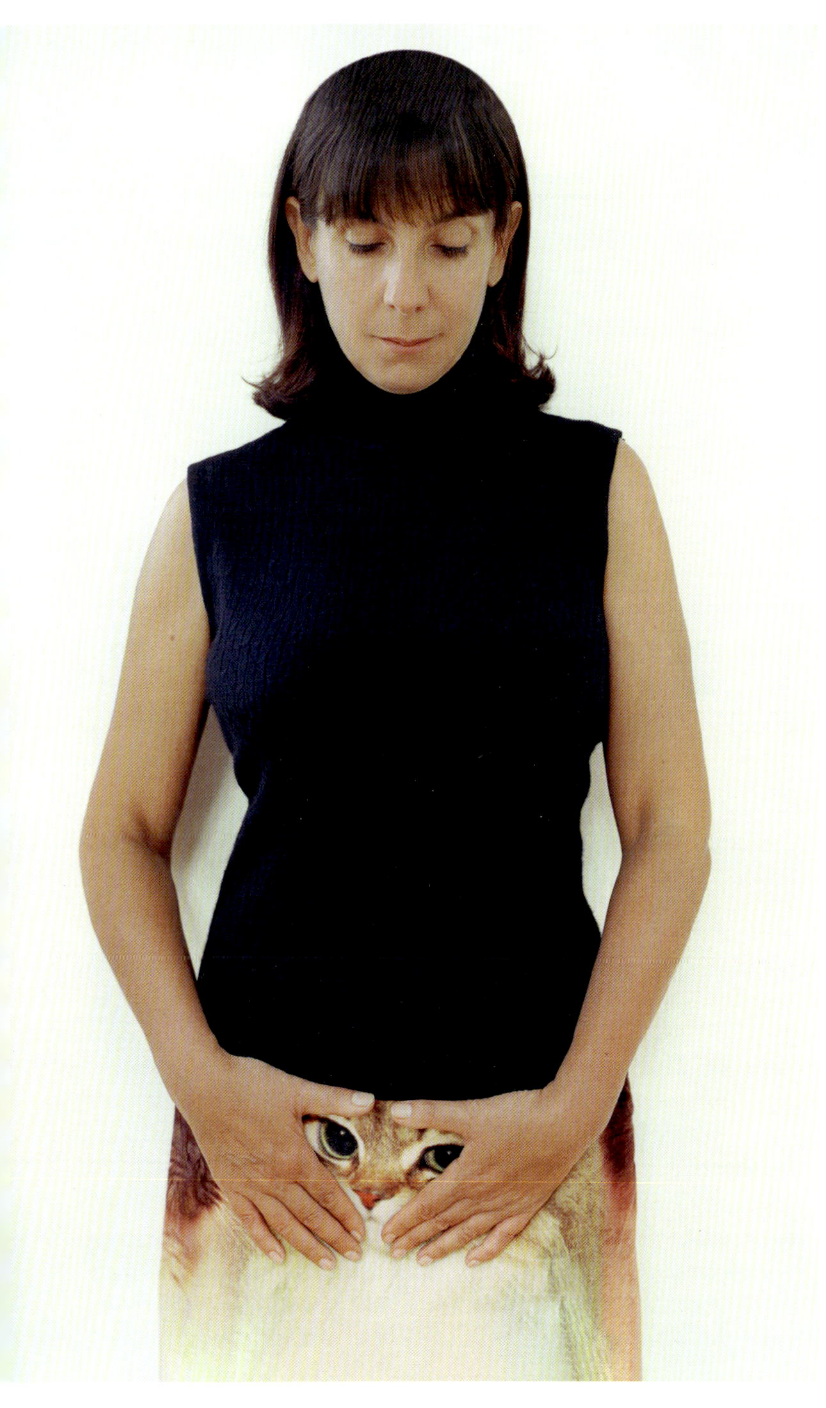

Shiner

My father, who planned everything, insisted that I shed no tears at his funeral. I held them back. The following night, half asleep, on my way to the garden I forgot to open the glass door and took his death smack in the face. I woke up with a black eye in the shape of a teardrop.

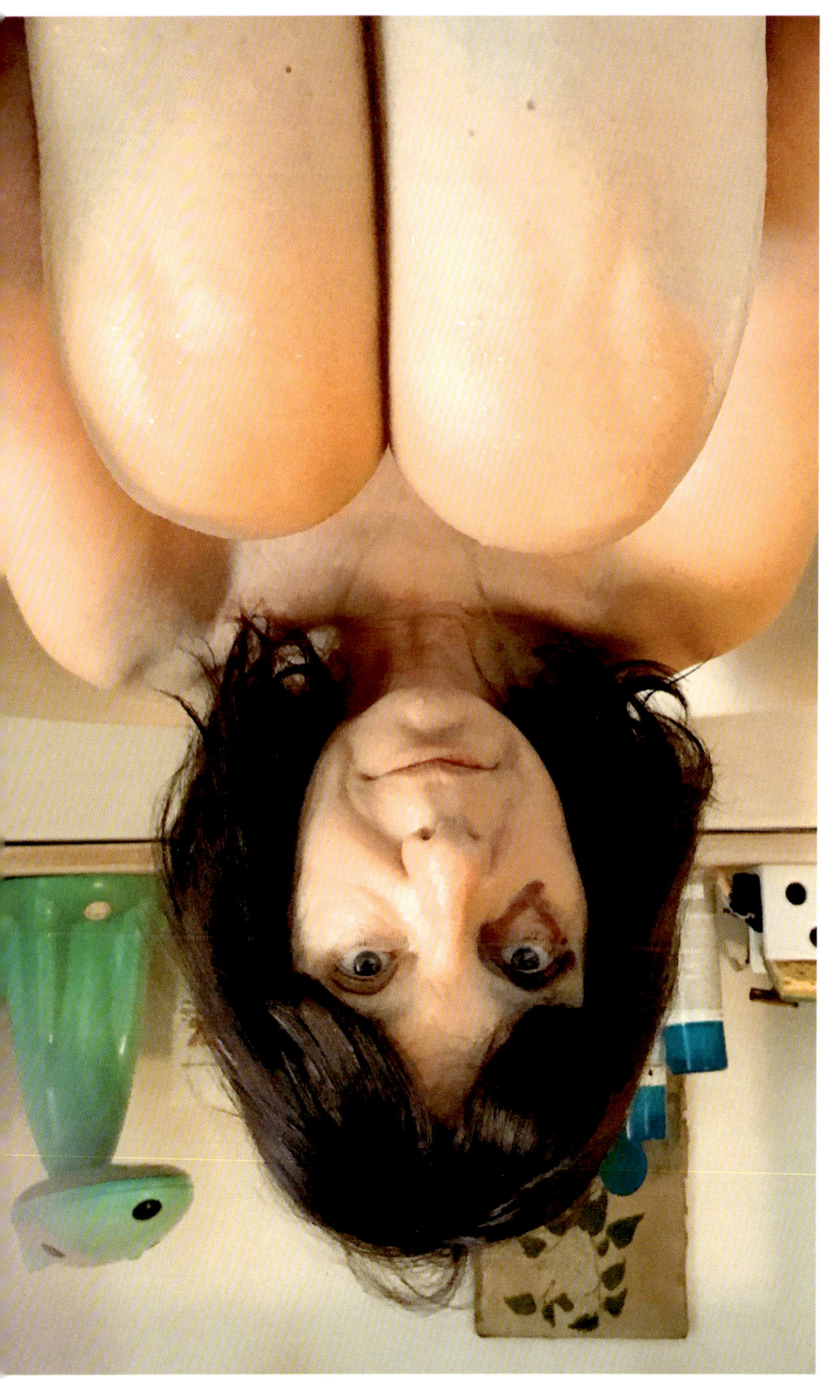

Plot

I purchased a plot in the Bolinas cemetery in California. The very same place where I took my first photographs. I would have liked to spend my death in the Montparnasse cemetery. But those who aren't dead yet cannot dream of taking up residency there. For this kind of real estate operation, you must die first. Difficult, in these conditions, to make plans to move in. During the purchase, since I live in France and there's a strong probability that I'll die there, I expressed concern about how my remains would reach California. The manager of the cemetery reassured me immediately: the body, by UPS; the ashes, by FedEx. This detail thus swept away, I became the owner of Lot 74, Section T, 8,949 kilometers away from Montparnasse.

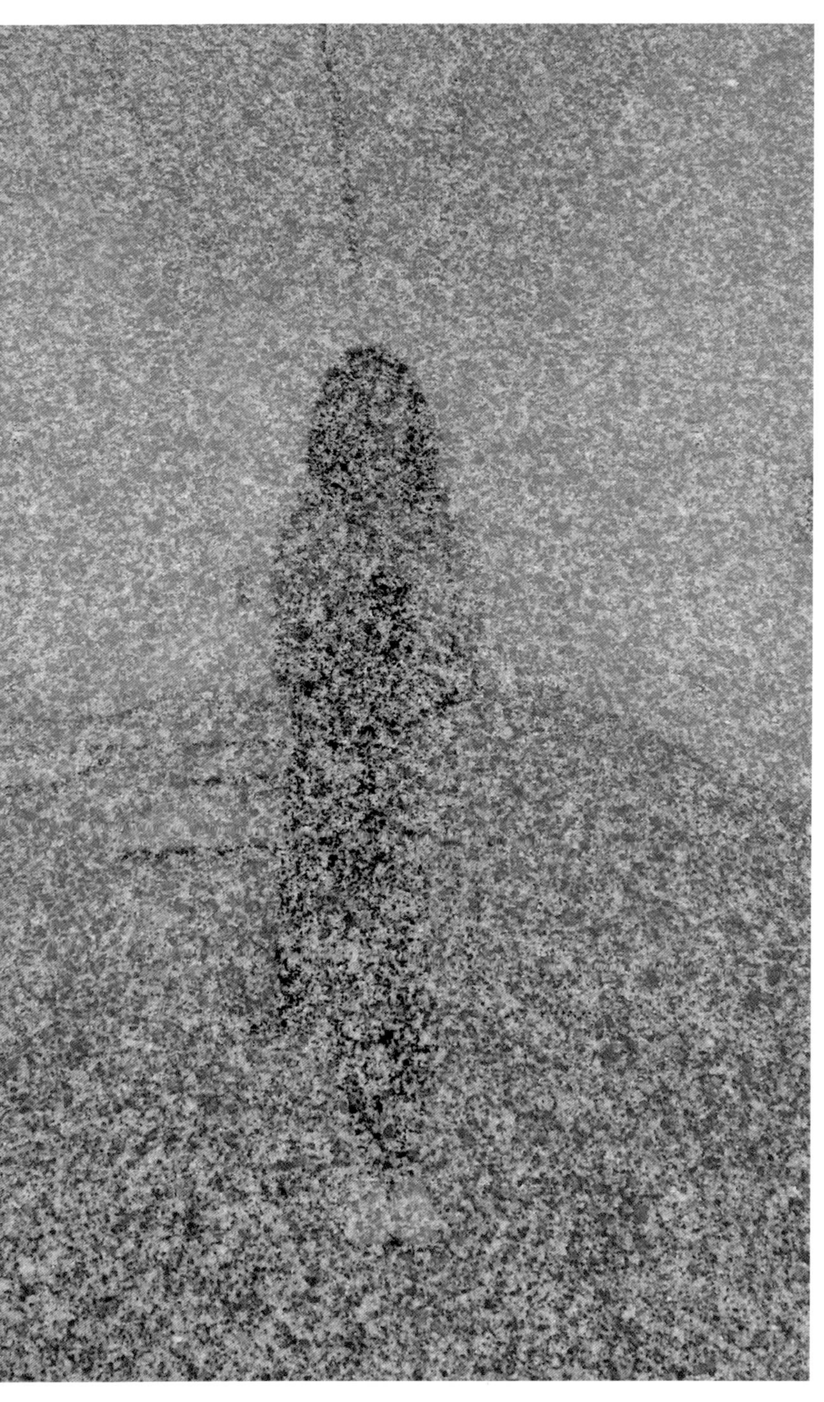

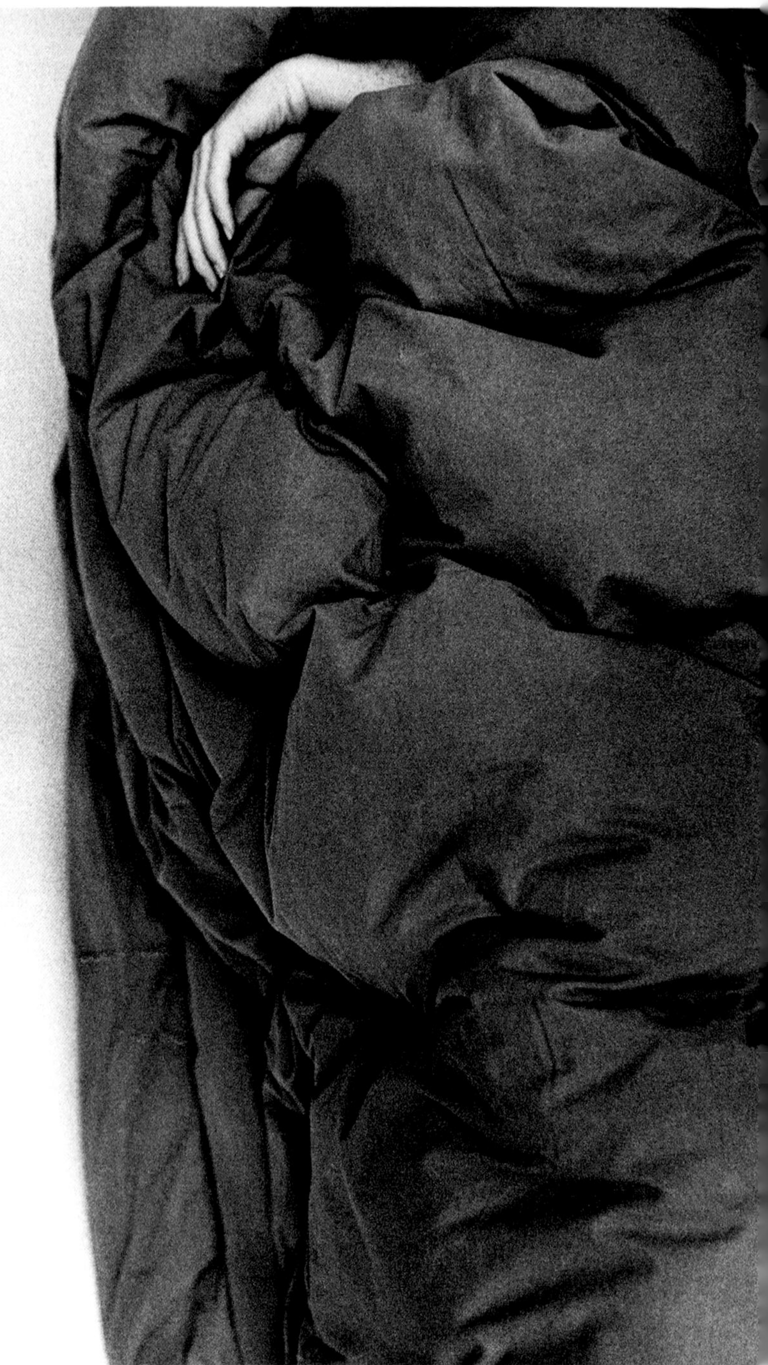

Night Stories

The Sleepers, 1979
The Hotel, 1981
Room with a View, 2002
Journey to California, 2003

The Sleepers

I asked people to give me a few hours of their sleep. To come and sleep in my bed. To let themselves be looked at and photographed. To answer questions. To each participant I suggested an eight-hour stay.

I contacted 45 people by phone: People I didn't know and whose names were suggested to me by common acquaintances, a few friends, and residents of the neighborhood whose work called on them to sleep during the day: the baker for instance. I intended for my bedroom to become a constantly occupied space for eight days, with sleepers succeeding one another at regular intervals.

29 people finally accepted. Among these five never showed up: an agency babysitter and I took their places. 16 people refused either because they had other commitments or the thing didn't agree with them.

The occupation of the bed began on Sunday, April 1 at 5 p.m. and ended on Monday April 9, at 10 a.m. 28 sleepers succeeded one another. A few of them crossed each other. Breakfast, lunch, or dinner were served to each depending on the time of day. Clean bedsheets were placed at the disposition of each sleeper.

I put questions to those who allowed me; nothing to do with knowledge or fact-gathering, but rather to establish a neutral and distant contact. I took photographs every hour. I watched my guest sleep.

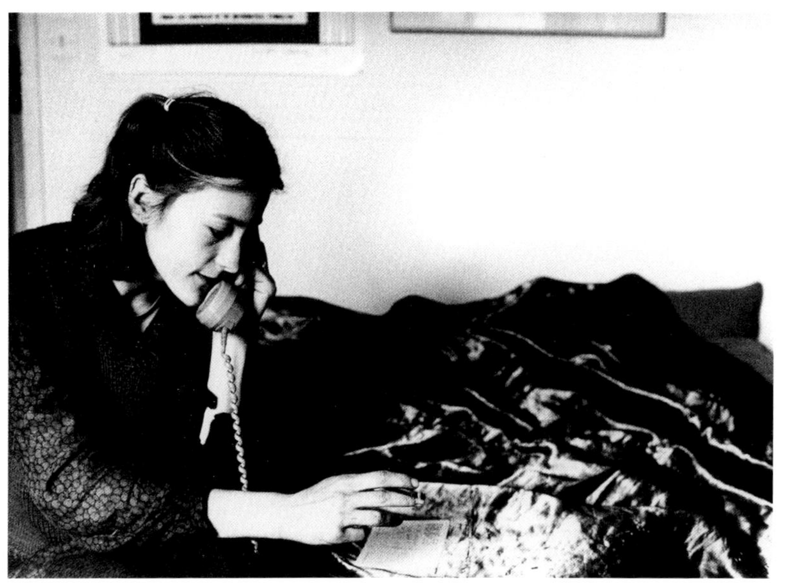

X, Babysitter, fourteenth sleeper

Thursday, April 6, at 11 a.m. I call Kid Service, a babysitting agency. They send me a young girl, whp turns up at 2 p.m. I describe my project to her. I ask her to sleep for me. She's worried. She's afraid that I'm a homosexual and that I'm going to attack her. She decides to stay, although the idea of going to bed repels her. She calls the man she's living with to ask him his opinion. He gives her permission to stay. She's relieved at having told him. She says that frees her from all responsibility. She gets into bed with her clothes on. (I changed the sheets just before her arrival.) She refuses all food and drink. She says she's tired but that it's out of the question for her to sleep. She agrees to answer my questionnaire. She relaxes. The crack in the wall and the postcards of nude women irritate her. At 5:10 p.m. she greets Fabrice Luchini. I leave them alone. At first their meeting is cordial but when she leaves at 6 p.m. she is annoyed. I see her out. I thank her for having changed her mind. I pay her. She tells me that she was very scared but that she doesn't regret having stayed. She adds that she's called Beryl.

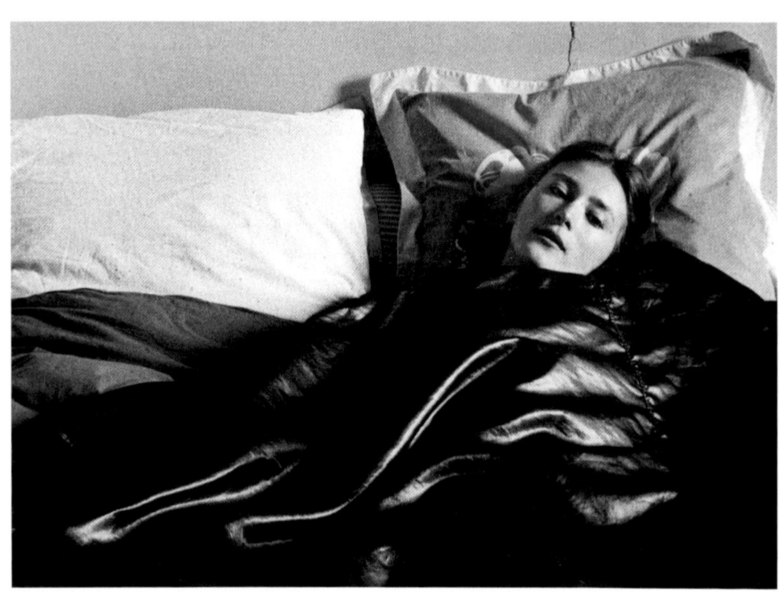

3:30 p.m. She tells me the story of a lesbian who pulled her into a tight hug, saying: "When you rest against my chest, darling, it won't be maternal."

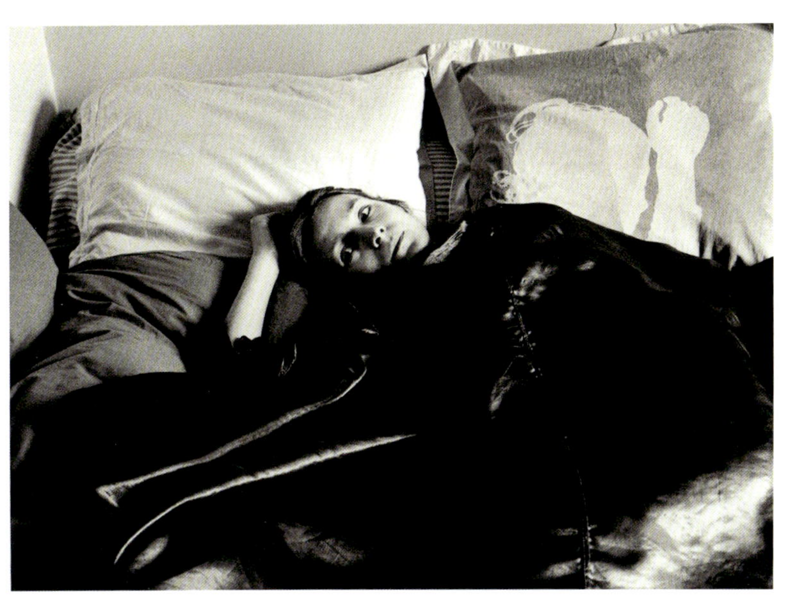

4 p.m. She says that she often dreams of blood and bombs.

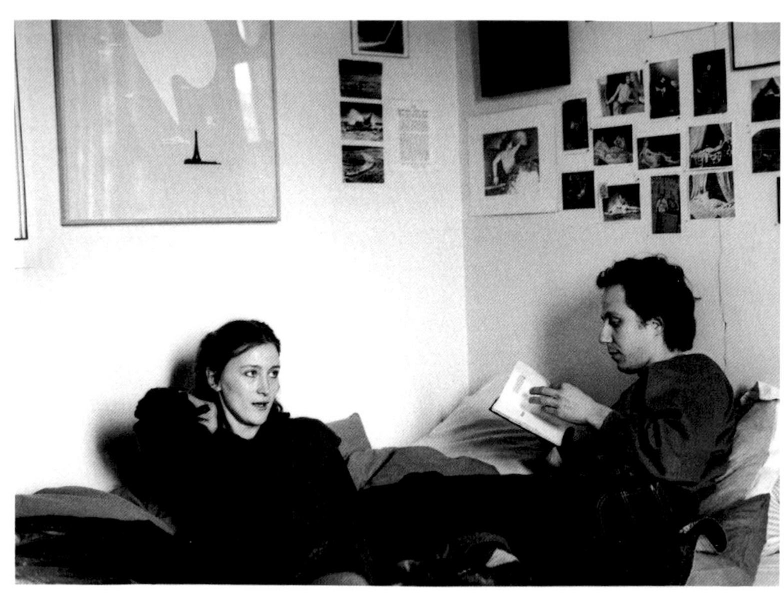

5:15 p.m. She meets Fabrice Luchini who is taking over from her.
She introduces herself: "I won't tell you my first name or surname.
I'm 25 years old, I'm a student." He invites her to share his sleeping time.

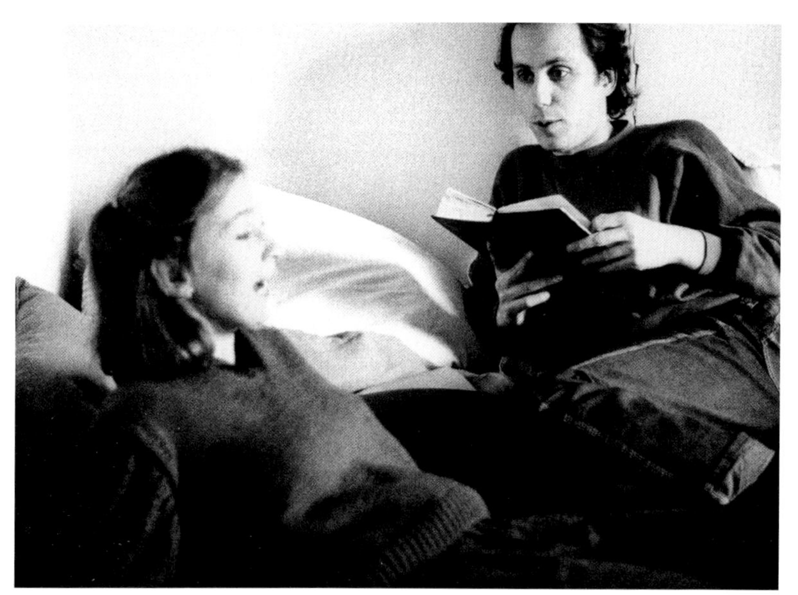

5:45 p.m. He makes her laugh.

At 6 p.m., she leaves.

The Hotel

On Monday February 16, 1981, I was hired as a temporary chambermaid for three weeks in a Venetian hotel. I was assigned twelve bedrooms on the fourth floor. In the course of my cleaning duties, I examined the personal belongings of the hotel guests and observed through details lives which remained unknown to me. On Friday March 6, the job came to an end.

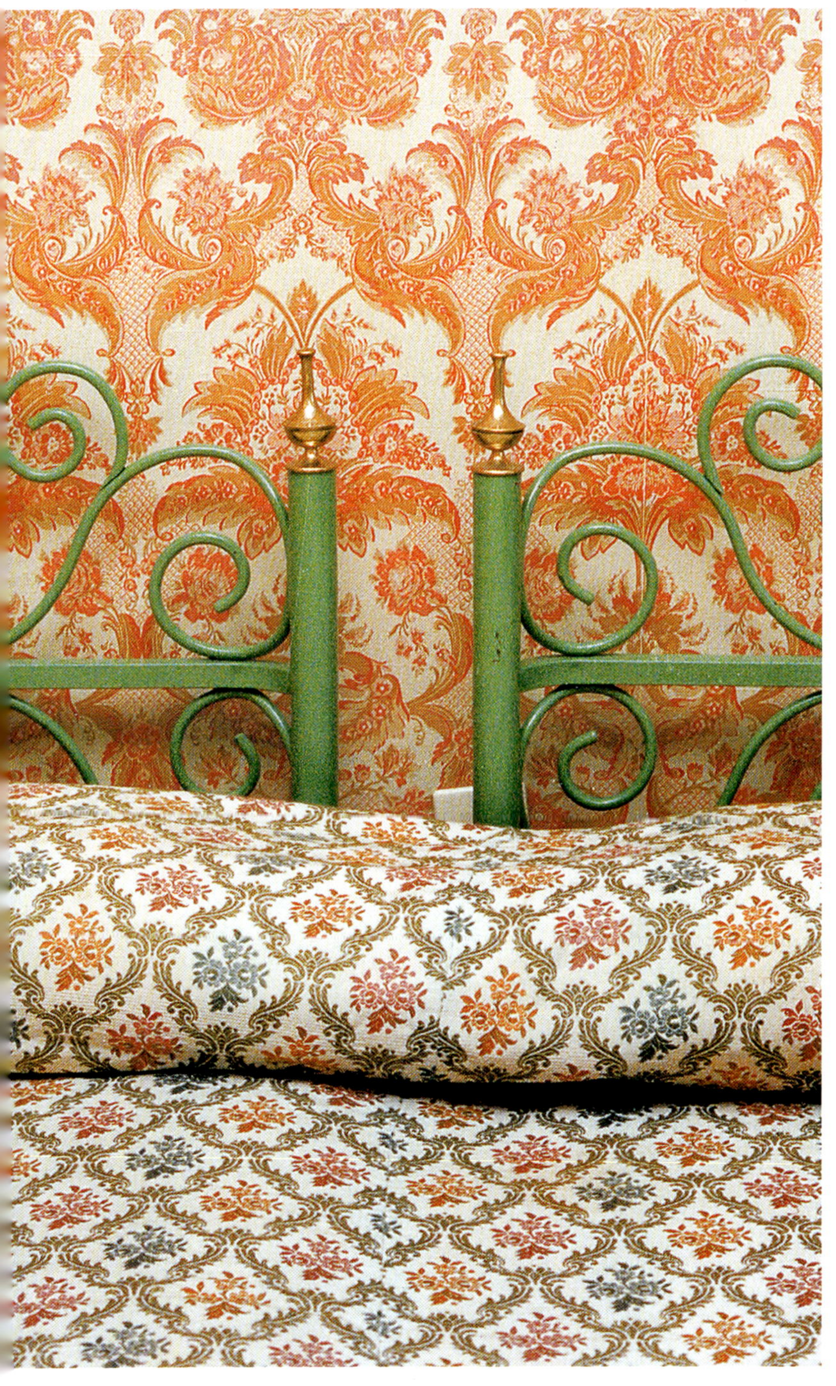

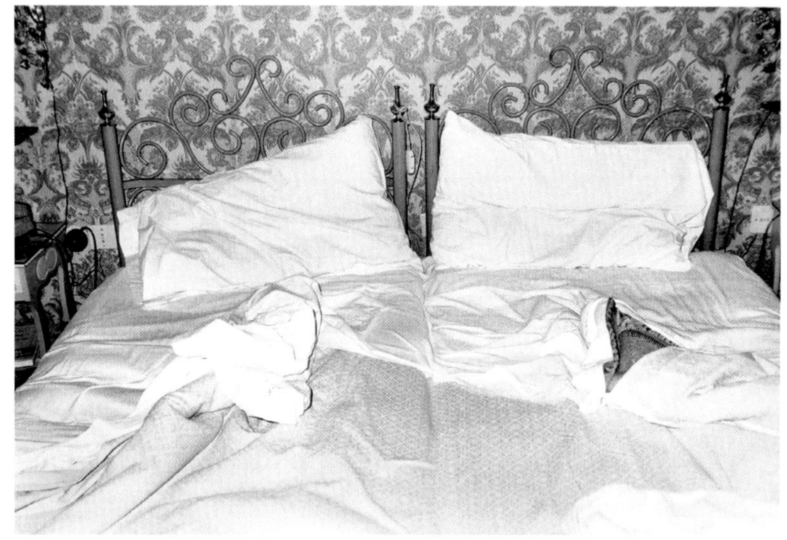

Room 30, February 24–27

Tuesday 24, 9:45 a.m. • I go into Room 30. The twin beds are unmade. A general disorder in the room, clothes are flung here and there: a pair of jeans, a suede jacket, etc. On the right-hand bedside table: maps of Venice, an alarm clock, a book, *Vendredi ou les Limbes du Pacifique* by Michel Tournier, an appointment book. I flip through it. For February 28, they have noted: "Return". For April 7: "Leave". On the "Notes" page: "See the Ghetto". The other pages are blank. The person on the left was smoking a cigar. On the bedside table, *Mishima* by Marguerite Yourcenar, a Minolta camera, and, in the drawer, an appointment book filled with notes. I'll look at this later.

In the wardrobe, a man's clothes: three pairs of trousers, four ties, two sweaters, a blue velvet suit. For the woman: a red dress, a gray skirt. The drawers are also full: socks, stockings, bras... very well equipped. Under the sweaters is a small, black, embroidered handbag. It contains 545 French francs, a dog-eared telegram, and a letter, a love letter. It is signed "Fabrice": "Wednesday evening. Dear Patricia: All of your little things plus a little sum of money in the wallet. The evening feels like paradise lost but I still feel happy because I have hope because you understand better than me what love is, what it entails. It's really a woman's business and I feel pretty clumsy about it all. This doesn't really count as a letter, I'll write you later. I love you, Patricia, and tell myself more and more how lucky I am to have found a woman like you. I kiss you very tenderly because you love it when I do that and so do I."

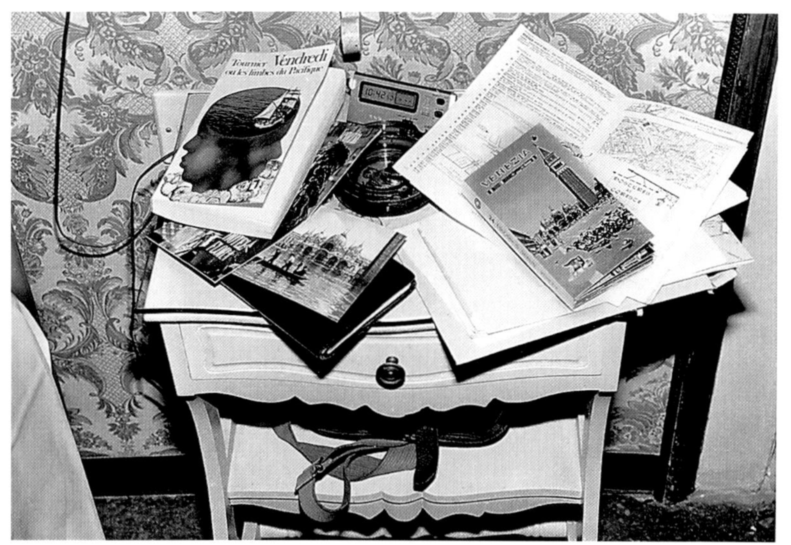

The telegram "What is going on darling?" had been sent from Chicago and addressed to Patricia [...], Paris, 11th *arrondissement*. It is signed by the same and dated October 25, 1965. [...]

Wednesday 25, 10:20 a.m. • On the bed, a newspaper, *Le Figaro*. Unusually, there are no pajamas. They have bought three nylon wigs and a pair of black mustaches for the carnival. On the table I find these few hand-written lines on a bit of paper: "He had remembered that look for you could not forget it." Not much work today. I sit on their bed and flip through the diary I glimpsed the day before It belongs to Patricia [...], a resident of the Paris suburbs and mother of two children [...]. Patricia belongs to a sports club, plays tennis, and is studying English. Her blood donor's card says: *Rhesus + O*. She was given an intravenous injection of 85 µg of anti-D immunoglobulin on 16.8.80. As for her engagements: *February 1: Antoine's wedding, bridge + dessert. February 3: Firemen. February 7: Anne at Maximilien's, Cub Scouts meeting, Brownies meeting... March 14: Cub Scouts meeting, Josselyn's wedding at 4 p.m. March 18: François. Coffee with the family. March 24: parish hall. March 27: Germaine Colas. 8:45 p.m.: CPM Donady team meeting. March 28: Brownies meeting. March 29: Cub Scouts outing. April 7: vacation.* For the next few days, there are also plans to go to the library with Gérard on May 11, on the 16th to the school party, and on June 19 there's the "meeting at home".

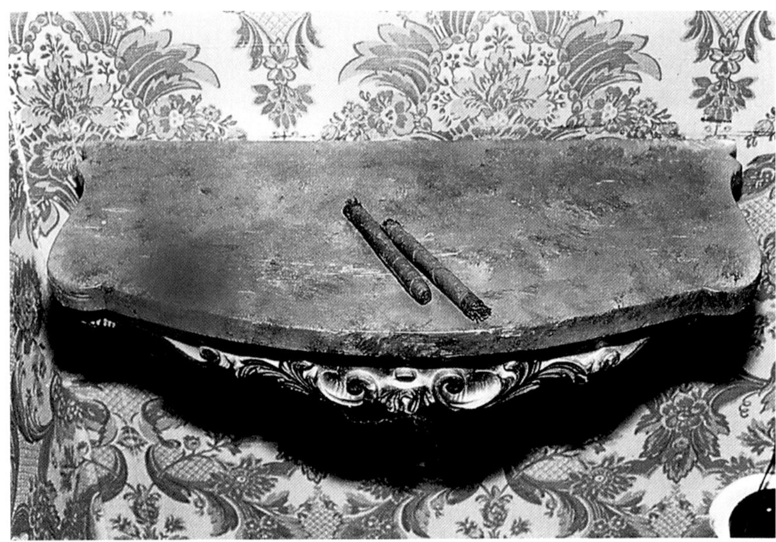

Between the pages of the diary I find a second letter. I read it: "My dear child, I am surprised not to have heard from you more often. I would love to know how you are. As for me, I am as well as can be expected. On March 5, I am going to the Senior Citizens Congress near Ales. There will be 5000 members from the Gard area. I also spent fifteen marvellous days in Rémusant, in the Drôme. Christmas day was brilliant. We had beautiful sunshine with an occasional drop of rain and went out to collect pine cones. Every day, I go for a good healthy walk on the hill. I'm still holding onto life and I hope to be able to write to you for a long time yet without rambling on. If you could see my courtyard in bloom you would be amazed: three camomiles as white as snow, six feet across, five or six pots of bright blue Carpathian campanula; the trailing geraniums, pink, red, mauve, and bright blue, have climbed up to the top of the palm tree, as have the nasturtiums. All this is incredibly colorful...

"I also wanted to tell you that Françoise's friend, the writer, Jeanne G, has died at ninety-four. Françoise says that Jeanne was messy. It's unbelievable, at her house they found forty umbrellas, seventeen overcoats, five or six furs, bundles of 10000-franc notes dating from 1914 to 1918. Quite a character. My dear, I enclose these lines with my letter. They're by Eliane Victor, the radio announcer, who recommends the MLF [Woman's Liberation Movement]. You should get yourself introduced there, get your foot in the door of a place where you could find a good, lucrative position. You don't push hard enough...

"I think I'll go to the nursing home soon. It might be fun. The sky would be the same as at home and the gardens are pleasant. The Bible says: 'Consider all things and take what is good.'

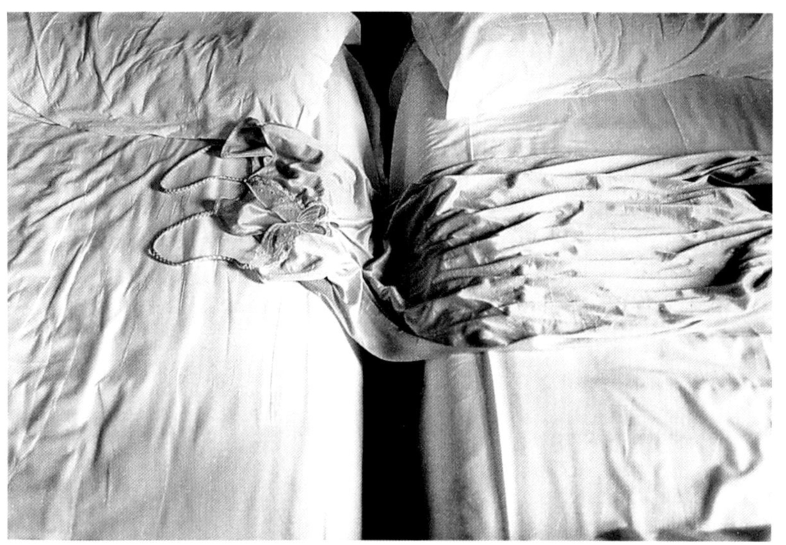

"I can't wait to see you. I hope that you soon tire of your travels. Valentine sends you hugs and kisses." [...]

Thursday 26, 10:20 a.m. • I'm in the hallway when the door of Room 30 opens. The occupant, a man, fortyish solidly built, with brown hair and a mustache, wearing a short bathrobe in terry cloth, holds his breakfast tray out to me and gives me a nice smile before closing the door of his room. Fabrice in the flesh? For the first time, I imagine for a few seconds a patron taking an interest in my plight as a chambermaid and telling me to drop everything and go away with him, to Paris perhaps. I notice that they drank the tea but ate nothing.

At 11:20 a.m. the couple leaves the room. I go in. An elegant nightshirt that I had not seen before is thrown across the two unmade beds like a bridge. The jeans are still in the same place over the back of the chair. They have bought a lot of postcards of paintings by Bellini, Veronese ... as well as a little embroidered cotton blouse for a child. I re-read the love letter and clean the room.

Friday 27, 10:20 a.m. • The suitcases of Room 30 have been put out in the hallway. They are leaving. I walk past them carrying my brooms and my pail. The man stops me; he says, "Thank you, this is from the whole floor," takes my hand and slips 33.50 francs into it.

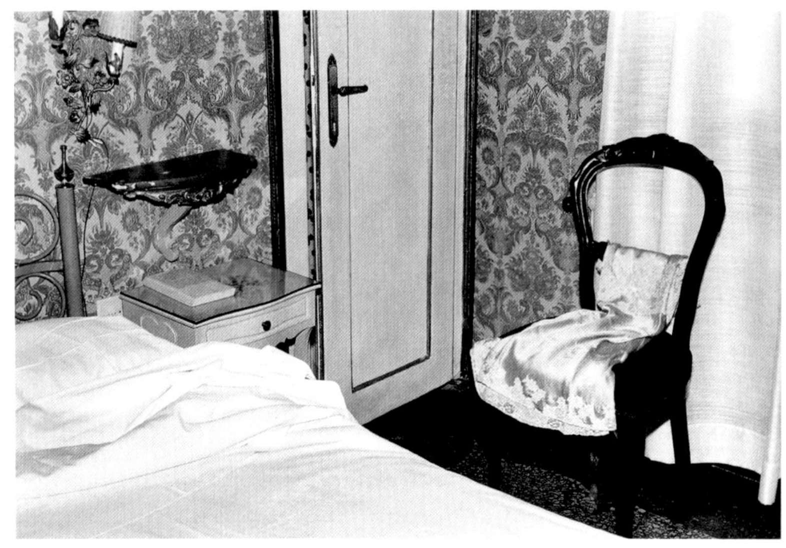

Room 30, March 4

Wednesday, March 4, 1981. 11:20 a.m. • I go into room 30. Only one bed has been slept in, the one on the right. There is a small bag on the luggage stand. A beautifully ironed silk nightgown lies on the chair that has been pulled up near the bed: it clearly has never been worn. Everything else is still in the traveling bag. All I see there is men's clothing: grey trousers, a grey striped shirt, a pair of socks, a toilet kit (razor, shaving cream, comb, aftershave lotion), a dog-eared photograph of a group of young people surrounding an older woman, a passport in the name of M.L., male sex, Italian nationality, born in 1946 in Rome, his place of residence, five foot seven, blue eyes. The bathroom is empty, so is the closet, but in the drawer of the night table, I find a box of Panter cigars, a fountain pen, airmail stationery, and a leather box with the initials M.L. On a piece of paper is the address of a Mr. and Mrs. B. in Florence, a wallet with five identical photographs of a blond woman and a wedding photograph showing the man in the passport in a tuxedo and the blond woman in a wedding gown. There is also an old bill from Hotel C., dated March 4, 1979, in the name of Mr. and Mrs. L for the same room, number 30. Exactly two years ago, M.L. spent the night in Hotel C. with his wife.

He has come back alone. With the embroidered nightgown in his suitcase. His reservation was for last night only. He is leaving today. I'll do the room later.

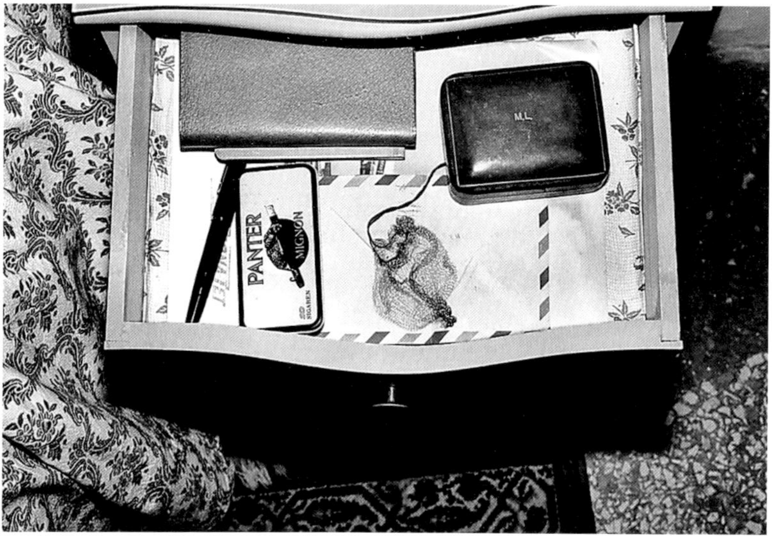

M.L.
PANTER
MIGNON
SIGAREN

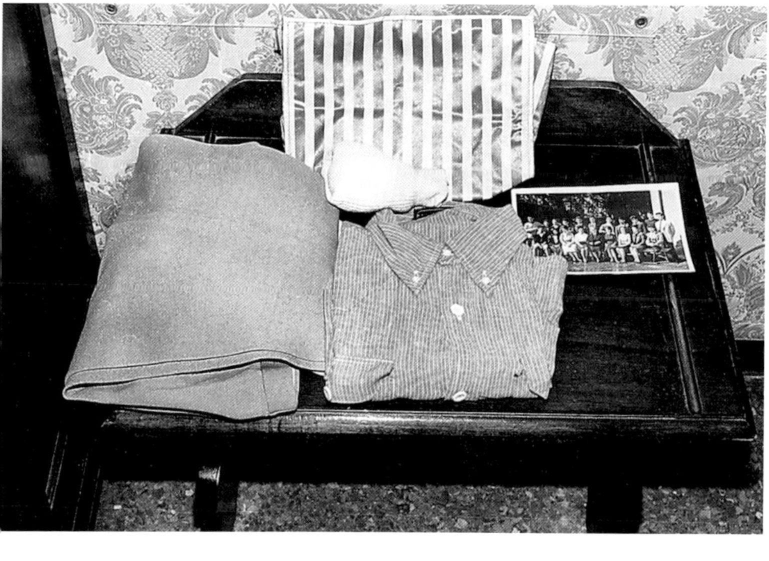

Room with a View

Some nights you can't put into words. I spent the night of October 5, 2002 in a room set up for me at the top of the Eiffel Tower. In bed. Between white sheets, listening to the strangers who took turns at my bedside. Tell me a story so I won't fall asleep. Maximum length: 5 minutes. Longer if thrilling. No story, no visit. If your story sends me to sleep, please leave quietly and ask the guard to wake me ... Hundreds turned up. Some nights you can't describe. I came back down in the early morning. A message was flashing on each pillar: *sophie calle, end of sleepless night, 7:00 a.m.* As if to confirm that I hadn't dreamt it all. I asked for the moon and I got it: I SLEPT AT THE TOP OF THE EIFFEL TOWER. Since then, I keep an eye out for it, and if I glimpse it along some street, I say hello. Give it a fond look. Up there, 1,014 feet above ground, it's a bit like home.

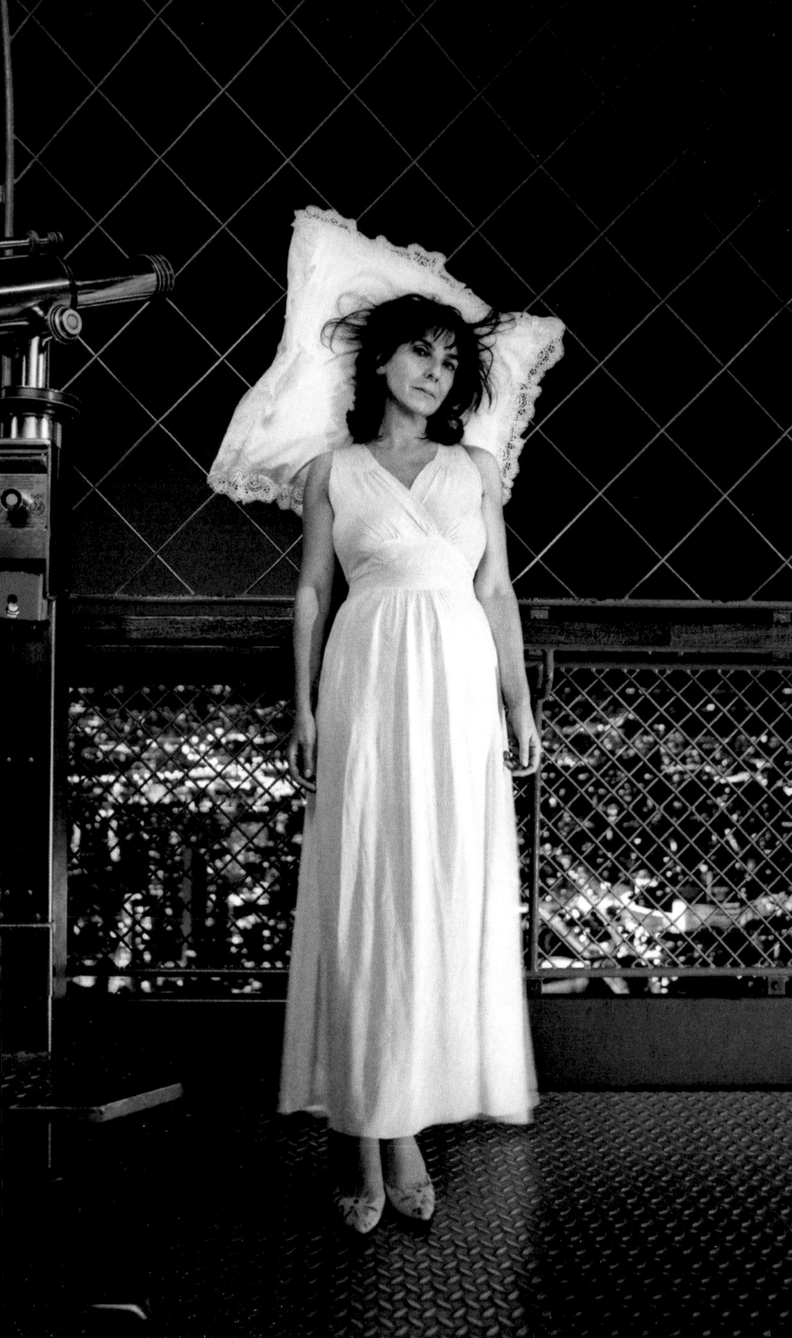

Journey to California

A man wrote to me from California: "June 4, 1999. Dear Ms. Calle, I have recently been released from a long-term relationship. I have been wading my way through various moods and emotions as a result of this separation. I would like to spend the remainder of my mourning/grieving period in your bed ..." How to say yes? Tricky. Considering how far he'd have to travel, would it be fair to send him packing if I found him unattractive? And besides, there was already a man in my bed. Two months later, my bed boarded the plane for San Francisco. The carrier delivered 1 bedstead, 1 box spring, 1 mattress, the sheets I had slept in, 2 pillows, 2 pillowcases and 1 blanket. I wished the recipient a quick recovery and urged him to keep me posted about his convalescence so I could reclaim my property once he had fully recovered. He acknowledged receipt of these items on August 4: "Your bed is very comfortable. I find the scent on the pillows and linen to be soothing. I will keep you abreast of my emotions and experiences ...".

In September, I heard that his pain had eased.

On February 2, 2000, my bed was back home.

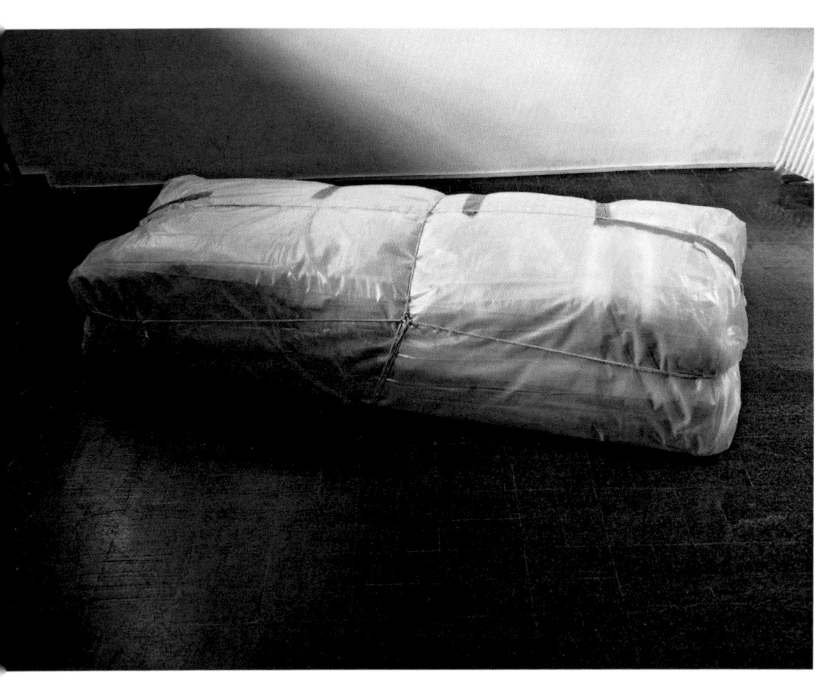

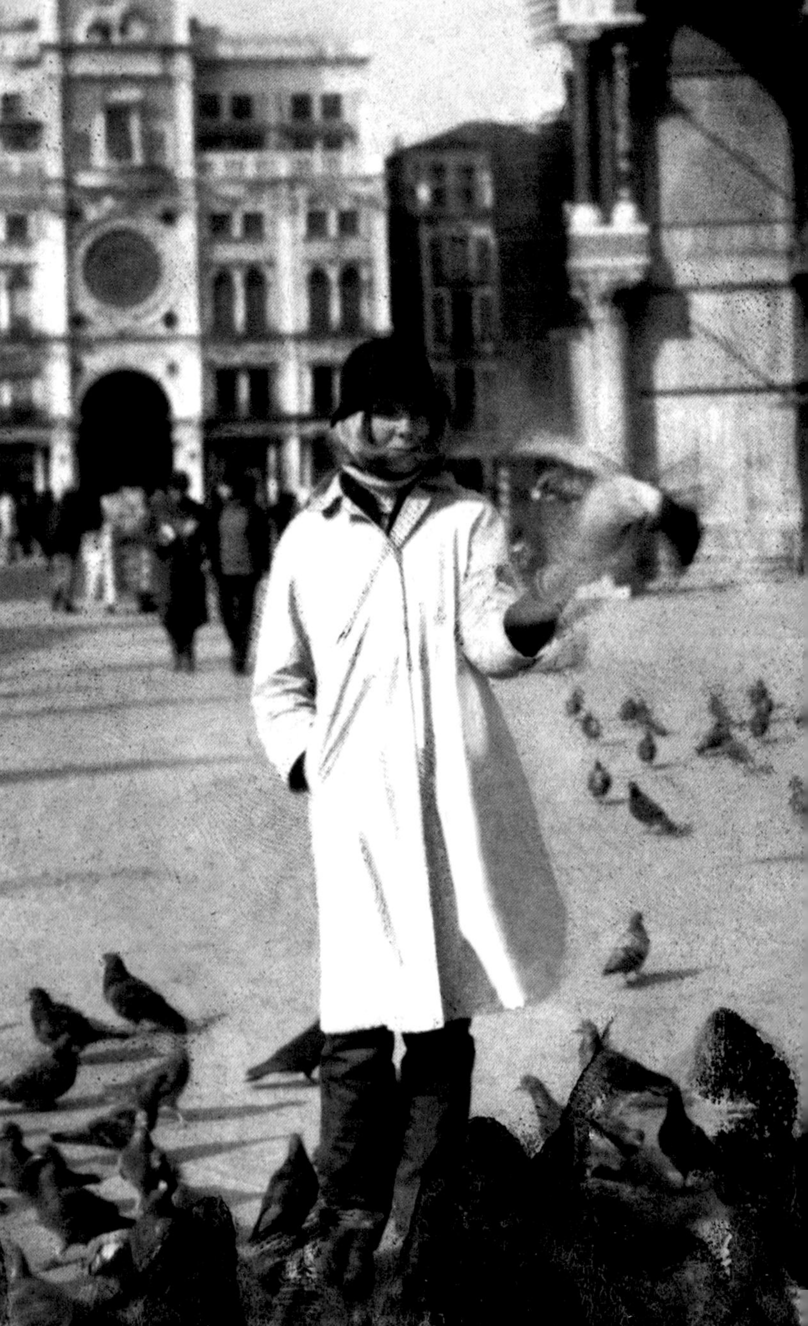

Wandering Stories

Suite vénitienne

At the end of January 1980, on the streets of Paris, I followed a man whom I lost sight of a few minutes later. That very evening, quite by chance, he was introduced to me at an opening. During the course of our conversation, he told me he was planning an imminent trip to Venice. I decided to follow him.

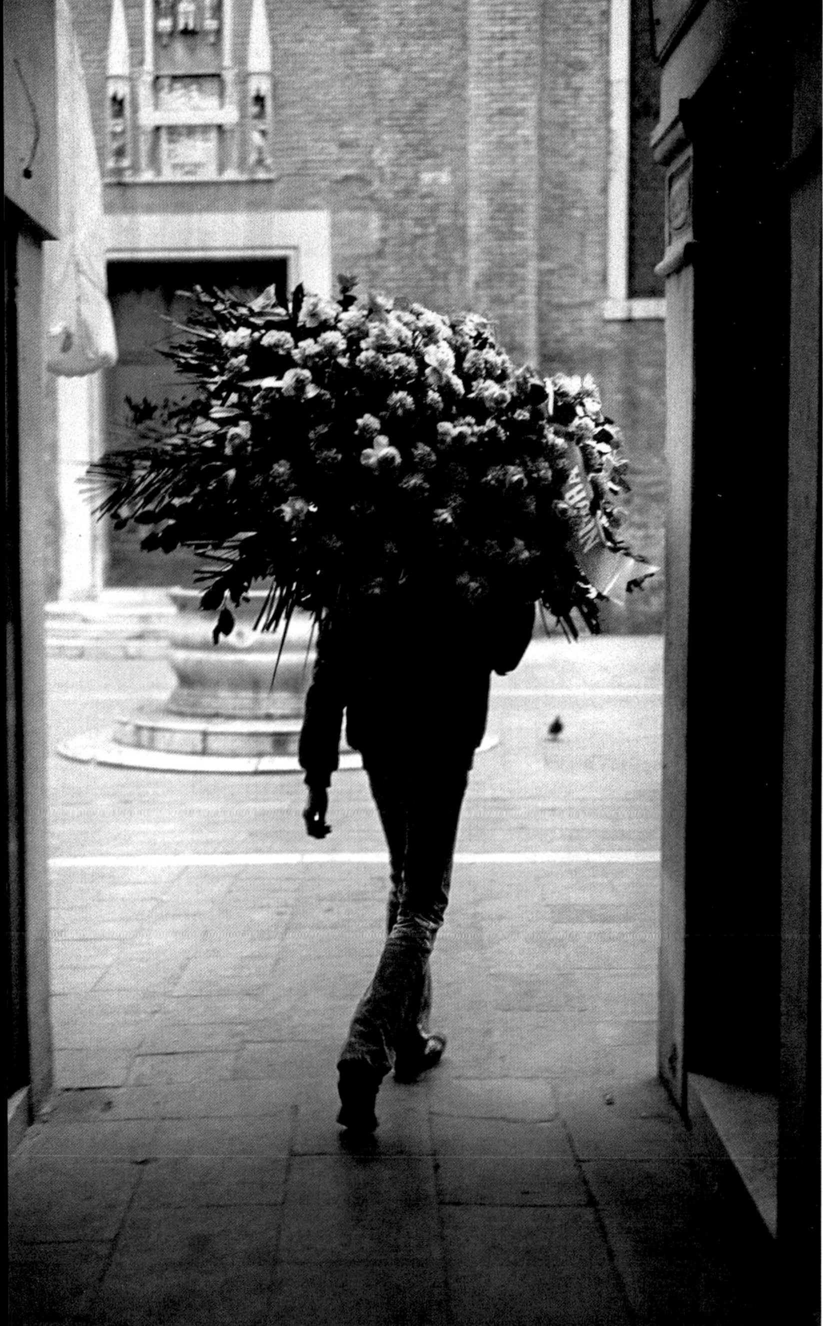

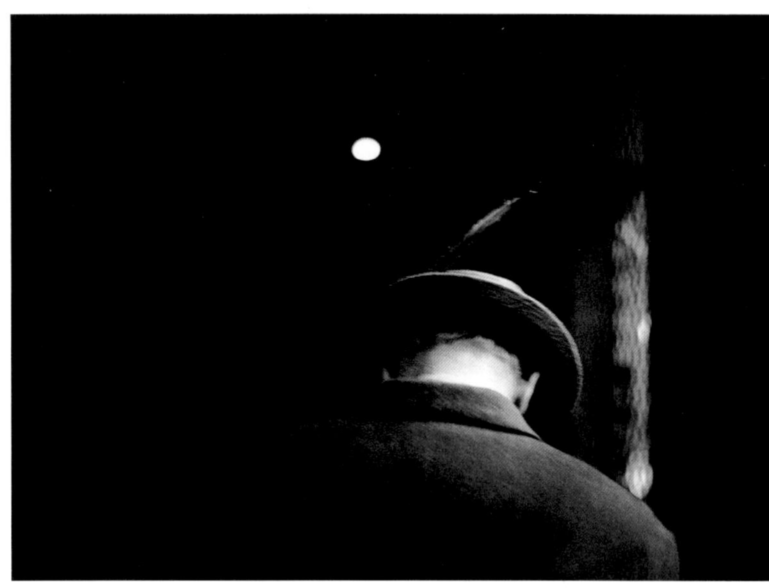

Monday. February 11, 1980

10:00 pm. Gare de Lyon. Platform H. Venice boarding area. My father
accompanies me to the platform. He waves his hand. In my suitcase:
a make-up kit so I can disguise myself; a blond, bobbed wig; hats; veils;
gloves; sunglasses; a Leica and a Squintar (a lens attachment equipped
with a set of mirrors so I can take photos without aiming at the subject).
I photograph the occupants of the other berths and then go to sleep.
Tomorrow I will see Venice for the first time.

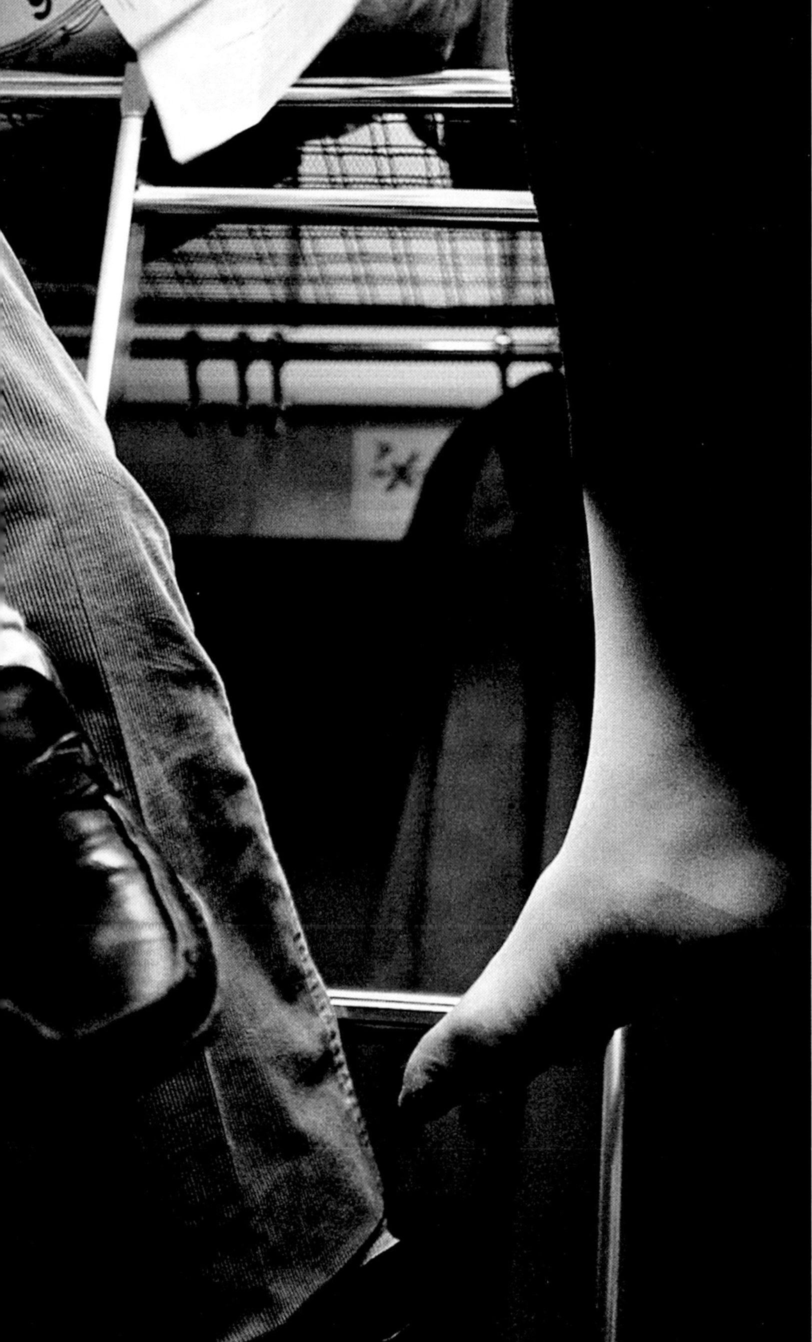

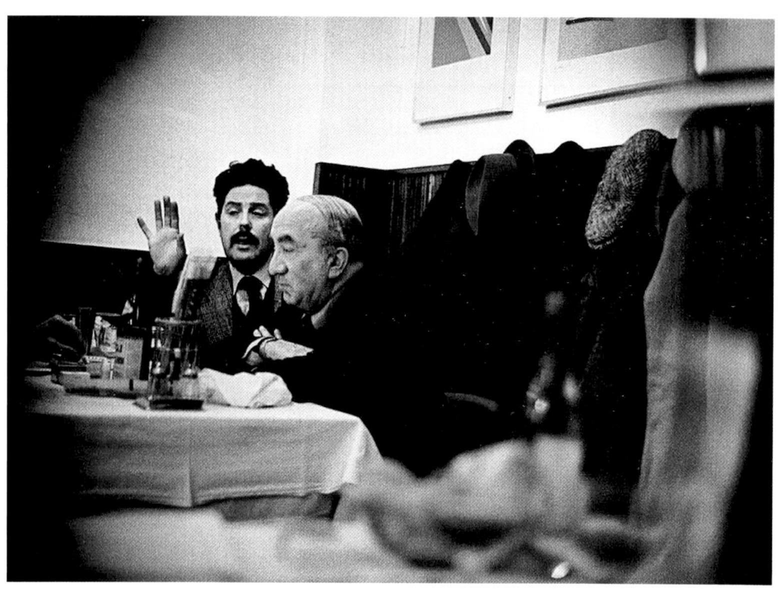

8:00 p.m. Dinner with Luciana C. at the restaurant Le Miliòn. For practice, while aiming at my friend, I photograph three men on my right with the Squintar.

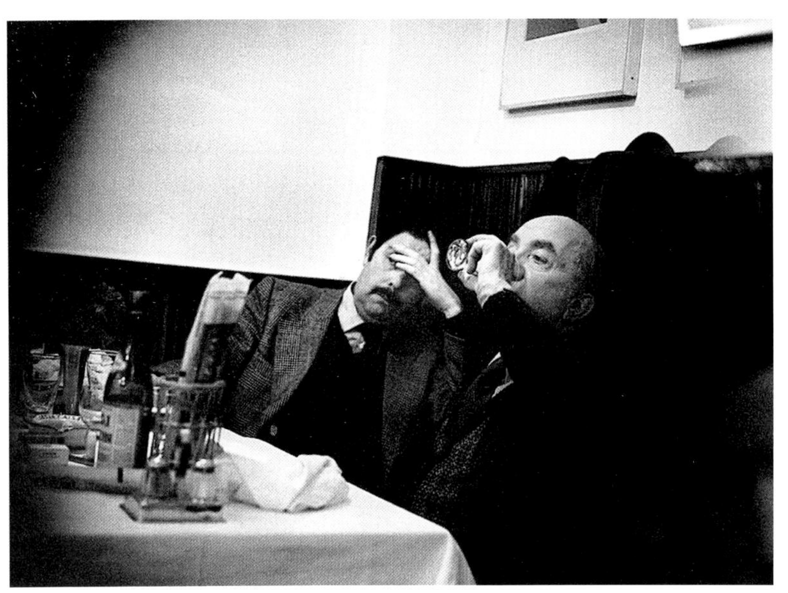

*The day Henri B. is there in front of me, will I be able to photograph him,
as well, while looking elsewhere? I doubt it.*
Midnight. I reach the pensione. I've been reciting his name since the
Ponte dell'Accademia. I remove my wig.
Today, for the first time in my life, someone called me a good-looking blond.

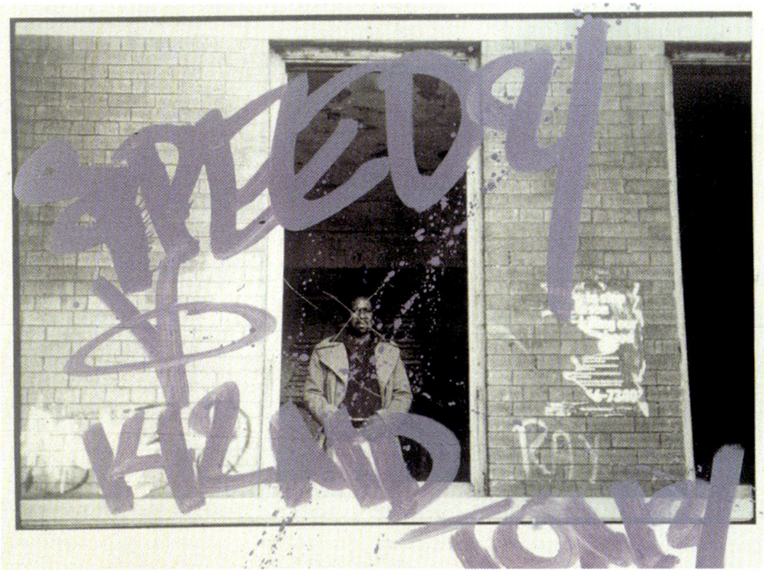

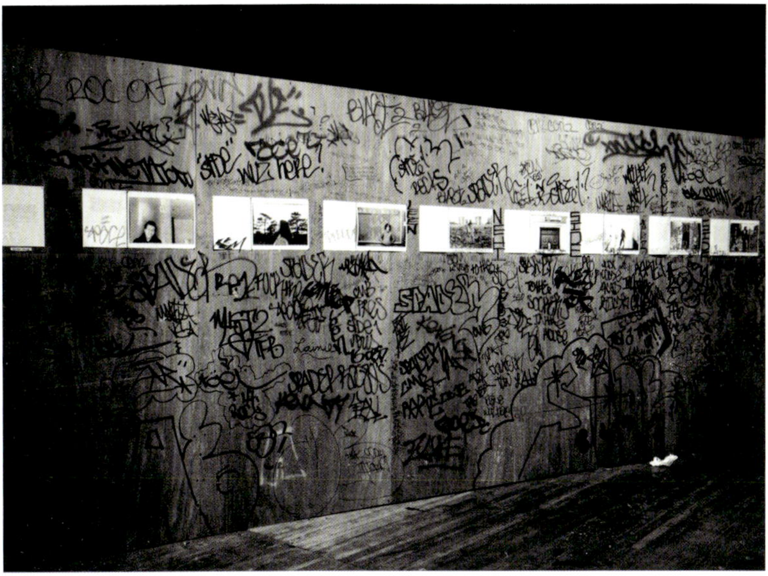

GREGORY
HELLAND
GREGORY

The Shadow

In April 1981, at my request, my mother went to a detective agency.
She hired them to follow me, to report my daily activities, and to
provide photographic evidence of my existence.

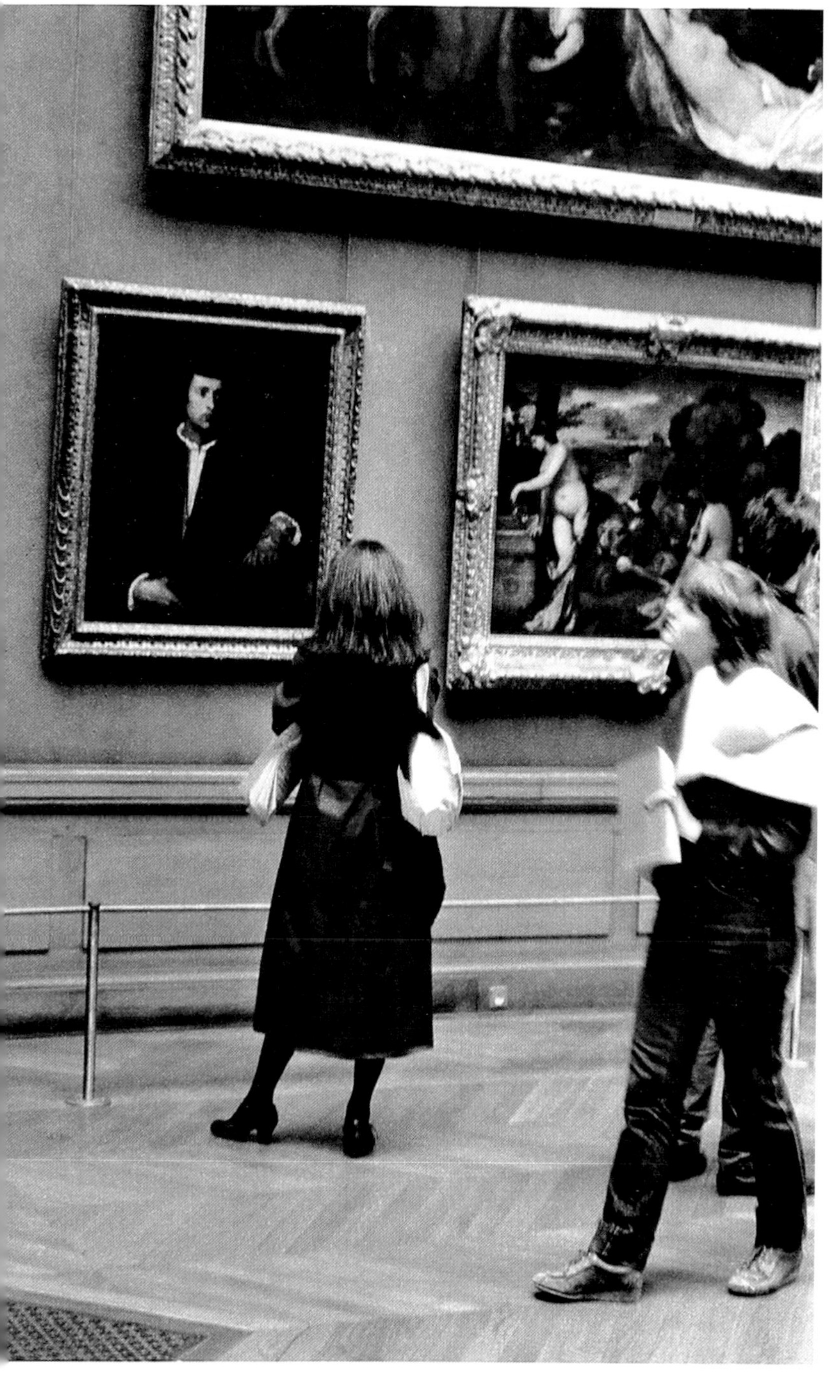

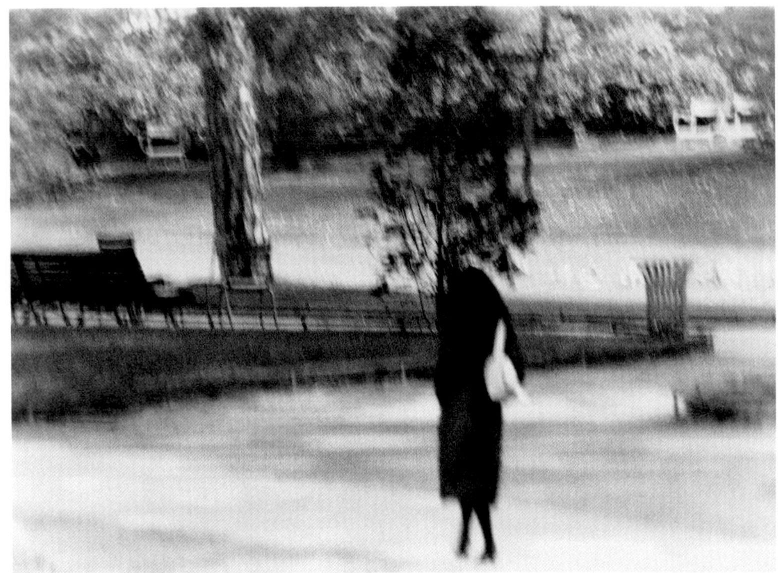

Thursday, April 16, 1981

At 10:00 a.m. I take up position outside the home of the subject, 22 rue Liancourt, Paris 14th.

At 10:20 the subject leaves home. She is dressed in a gray raincoat, gray trousers, and wears black shoes with stockings of the same color. She carries a yellow shoulder bag.

At 10:23 the subject buys some daffodils at the florist's on the corner of rue Froidevaux and rue Gassendi, then enters Montparnasse cemetery at 5 rue Emile-Richard. She lays the flowers on a tomb then leaves the cemetery on the boulevard Edgar-Quinet side.

At 10:37 the subject buys a newspaper from the stand at 202 boulevard Raspail.

At 10:40 she enters 100 boulevard Montparnasse.

At 11:32 the subject comes out of the building in the company of a friend aged approximately twenty-seven, height 5' 5", of very stout build, long brown hair, wearing light brown trousers and a black sweater.

At 11:38 the subject says goodbye to her friend outside 21 rue Delambre and enters the Jacques Guérin hair salon.

At 12:08 the subject leaves the salon and crosses the Jardin du Luxembourg and appears to wait outside Odéon metro station.

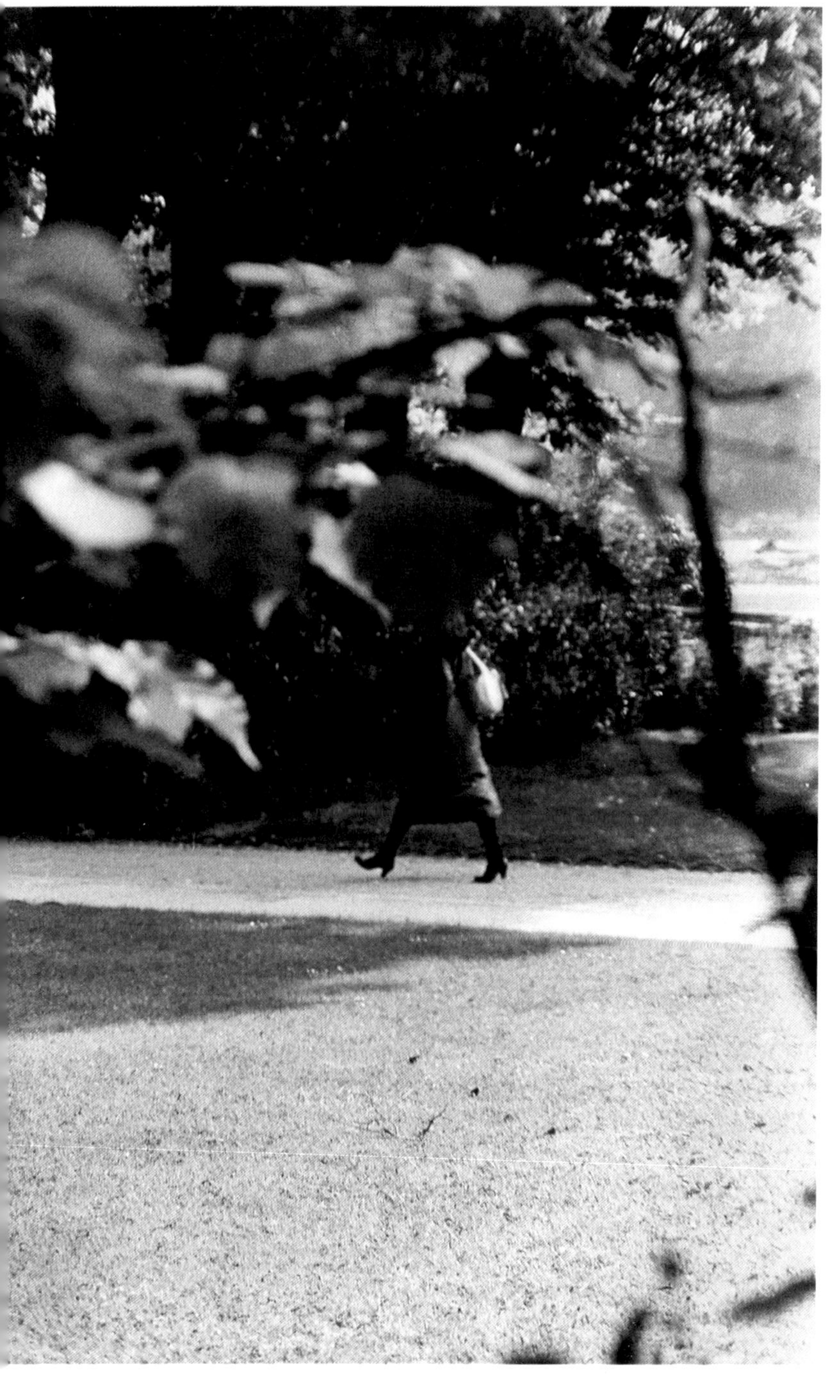

The Address Book

In June 1983, I found an address book. I photocopied the contents then
sent it back anonymously to its owner, whose address was written on the
endpaper. Since *Libération* had asked me to do an instalment piece for
publication in the newspaper that same summer, I decided to contact
some of the people whose names appeared in the book and ask them
to tell me about the owner. Through them, I would get to know this man.

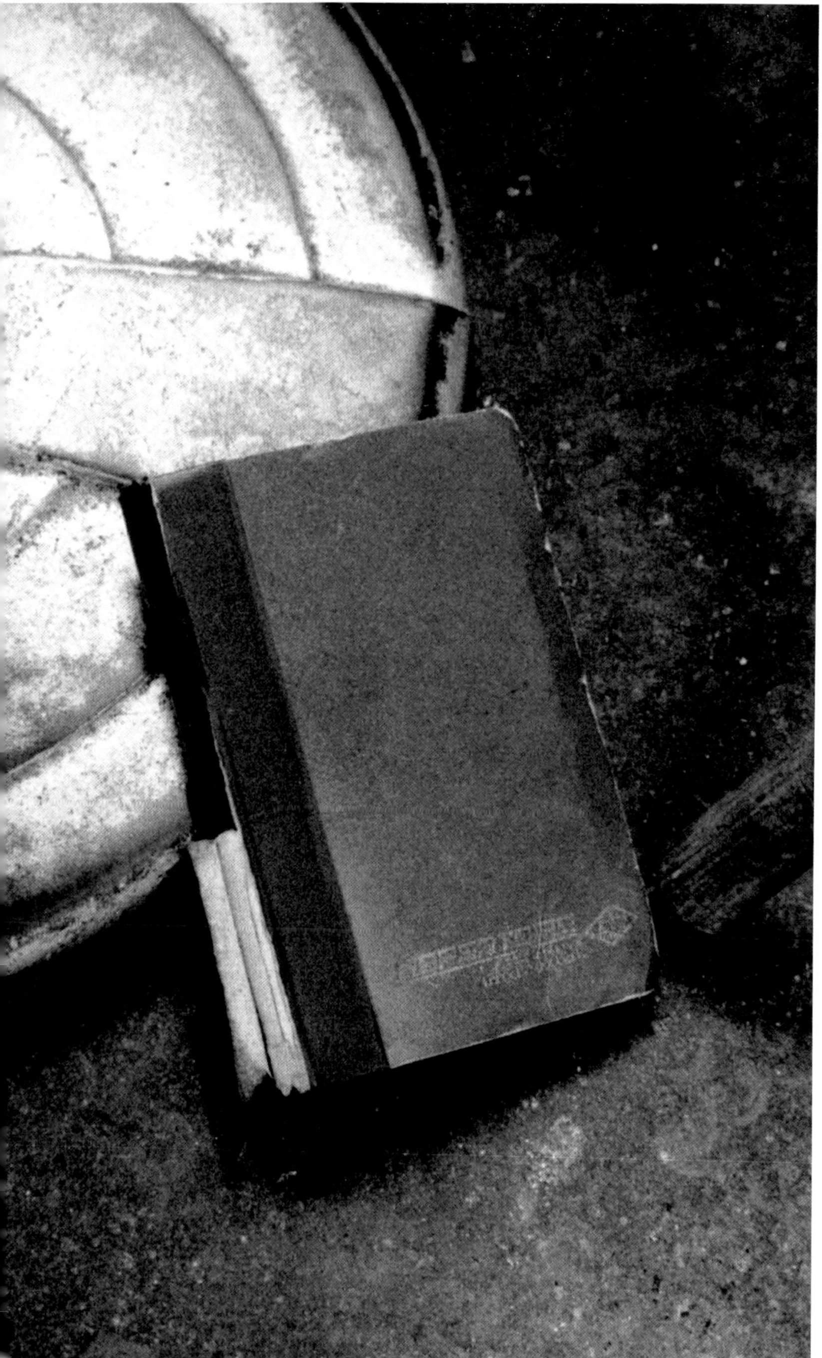

prévenance à l'égard des enquêteurs.
Depuis le 5 juillet, date de sa disparition, les gendarmes étaient à la recherche de Jean-Claude Kaiserlian.

méprendre à la photo diffusée dans toute la presse après le double meurtre du bois de Païolive, en avril dernier : cheveux bruns, yeux noirs,

l'AFP) qui l'a connu à cette époque, Pascal Blanc est alors « un garçon calme et sans problème, à tel point qu'il avait été choisi par ses camarades

Pascal Blanc lui reproche sa « dureté » et peut-être aussi d'avoir fermé le centre où il avait passé dix années de son enfance. Un meurtre signé en tout cas,

d'homicides volontaires ou d'assassinats sur les personnes d'Isabelle Alison et de Philippe Vigneron, les deux jeunes campeurs du bois de Païolive.

L'HOMME AU CARNET

Le feuilleton de l'été, liant textes et images, commence aujourd'hui. L'enquête de Sophie Calle se poursuivra durant plus d'un mois pour dresser le portrait d'un inconnu.

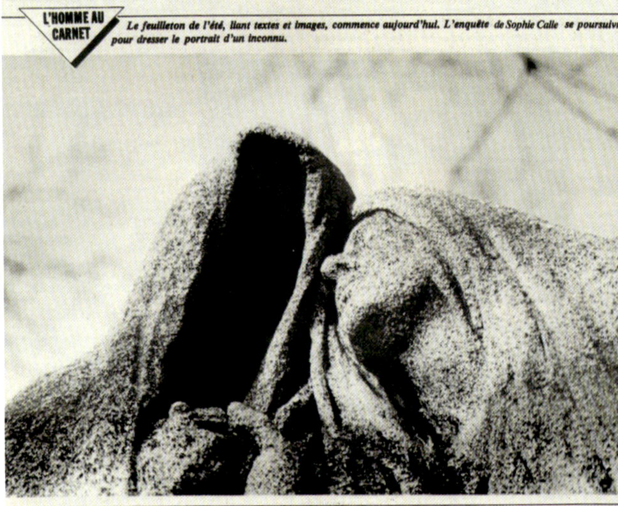

PARIS.
Fin juin.

Je trouve un carnet d'adresses par terre. Je le ramasse. Quelques heures plus tard je le renvoie, anonymement, à son propriétaire dont les coordonnées sont indiquées sur la première page. Entre temps je l'ai entièrement photocopié. J'appellerai ceux qui figurent dans le carnet. Je leur dirai : « J'ai trouvé un carnet d'adresses par hasard dans la rue. J'ai vu votre nom et j'aimerais vous rencontrer ». Je leur demanderai de me parler du propriétaire du carnet dont je ne dévoilerai le nom qu'au moment de l'entretien, s'ils m'accordent un rendez-vous. J'approcherai cet homme à travers ses amis, les descriptions qu'ils me feront de lui. J'apprendrai à le connaître. Il s'appelle Pierre D.

---

d'un calibre supérieur aux trois hommes déjà connus : Jean Roussel, arrêté sur place, Jacques Gouttenoire, abattu le lendemain, et Christian Paris, en cavale. Autant dire que malgré le silence, et même les dénégations des enquê-

compagnent leur maître. La cour, ombragée de chênes verts paraît à l'abandon et le poney noir lève à peine son œil morne sur les visiteurs. Tout le monde pénètre dans la maison. « Simple vérification » lance un inspecteur

tue et tranchante et déclare qu'un couteau ensanglanté aurait été retrouvé.

Mais cela s'est-il passé avant ou après le coups de feu qui leur ont éclaté la tête ? En tous cas, ce détail noircit le film de

deux jours auparavant en Conseil des Ministres, notamment celles concernant « le seuil de 14 ans, à partir duquel même un détenu condamné à perpétuité pourra sortir ».

« Sur le plan concret, la responsabili-

éventuellement examiner avec plus d'attention par un tribunal la manière dont sont accordées les permissions. Quant au fameux seuil de 14 ans, il sert, au contraire, lui aussi, à codifier de manière plus restrictive une pratique déjà existante...

L'HOMME AU CARNET

Paris. Fin juin, rue des Martyrs. Je trouve un carnet d'adresses. Je le ramasse, le photocopie et le renvoie, anonymement, à son propriétaire. Il s'appelle Pierre D. Je demanderai à ceux qui figurent dans le carnet de me parler de lui. Je l'approcherai, chaque jour, par leur intermédiaire.

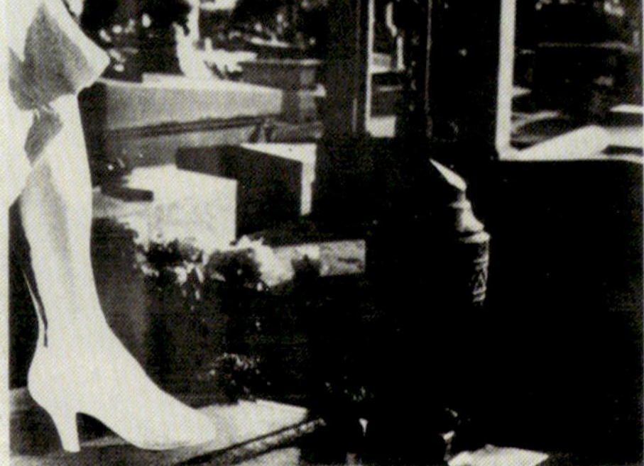

**MARDI- Florence B.
14 h 30- 15 h 30**

Une odeur ? « Oui, celle du cigare, me fait penser à lui ».

Elle dit que Pierre l'intrigue : « Ce qui me fascine le plus, c'est la façon dont il parle, le nez pointé en l'air comme s'il humait ce qui se passe ».

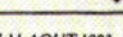

Paris. Fin juin, rue des Martyrs. Je trouve un carnet d'adresses. Je le ramasse, le photocopie et le renvoie, anonymement, à son propriétaire. Il s'appelle Pierre D. Je demanderai à ceux qui figurent dans le carnet de me parler de lui. Je l'approcherai, chaque jour, par leur intermédiaire.

JEUDI-CHARLY T. 9h-10h15

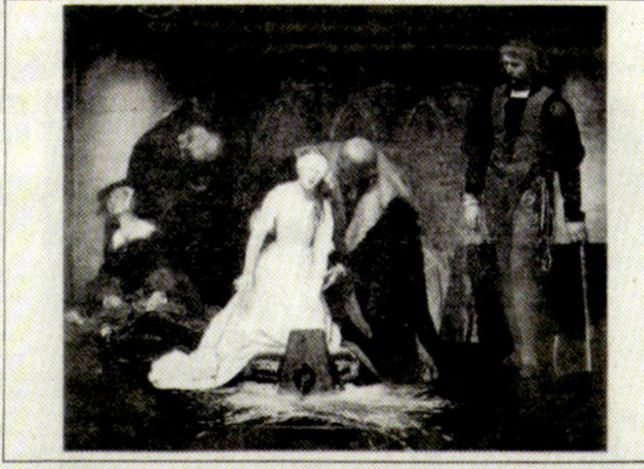

Il dit qu'il peut me raconter le genre de blague que Pierre D. adore, et plus particulièrement celle-ci, qui le fit mourir de rire en 1970 : « C'est l'histoire d'un jeune homme qui fait un sondage sur la vie sexuelle des Français : - Pardon, Madame, pourriez-vous m'indiquer les zones érogènes ? Et la dame répond : - Excusez-moi, je ne suis pas du quartier ». Charly T. doit partir. Il propose de me prêter une carte postale que

Pierre lui avait envoyée de Londres.

Je la reçois le lendemain. Il s'agit d'une peinture de Paul Delaroche, « The execution of Lady Jane Grey », 1909, National Gallery.

SOPHIE CALLE

Paris. Fin juin, rue des Martyrs. Je trouve un carnet d'adresses. Je le ramasse, le photocopie et le renvoie, anonymement, à son propriétaire. Il s'appelle Pierre D. Je demanderai à ceux qui figurent dans le carnet de me parler de lui. Je l'approcherai, chaque jour, par leur intermédiaire.

SAMEDI
Paul B 12h30 13h30

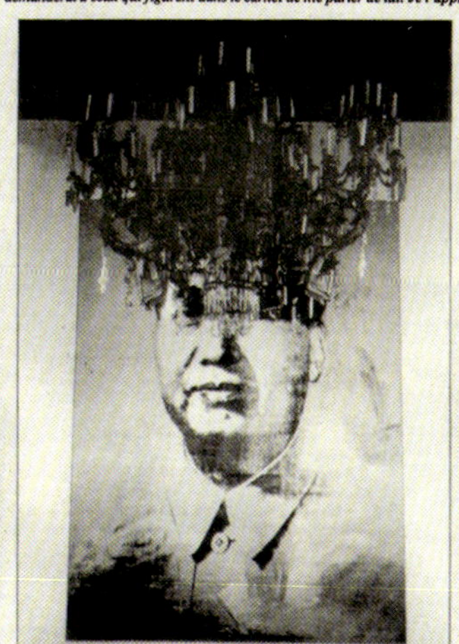

Il avait cet avantage qu'on n'a pas su exploiter, c'est de s'intéresser aux films burlesques...

Pierre lui avait dit : « Reste là. Ne me quitte pas. J'ai très peur dans l'avion ».

- Quelle est l'image qu'il a de lui ? « Celle d'un enfant qu'on a oublié dans un aéroport. »

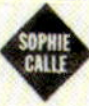

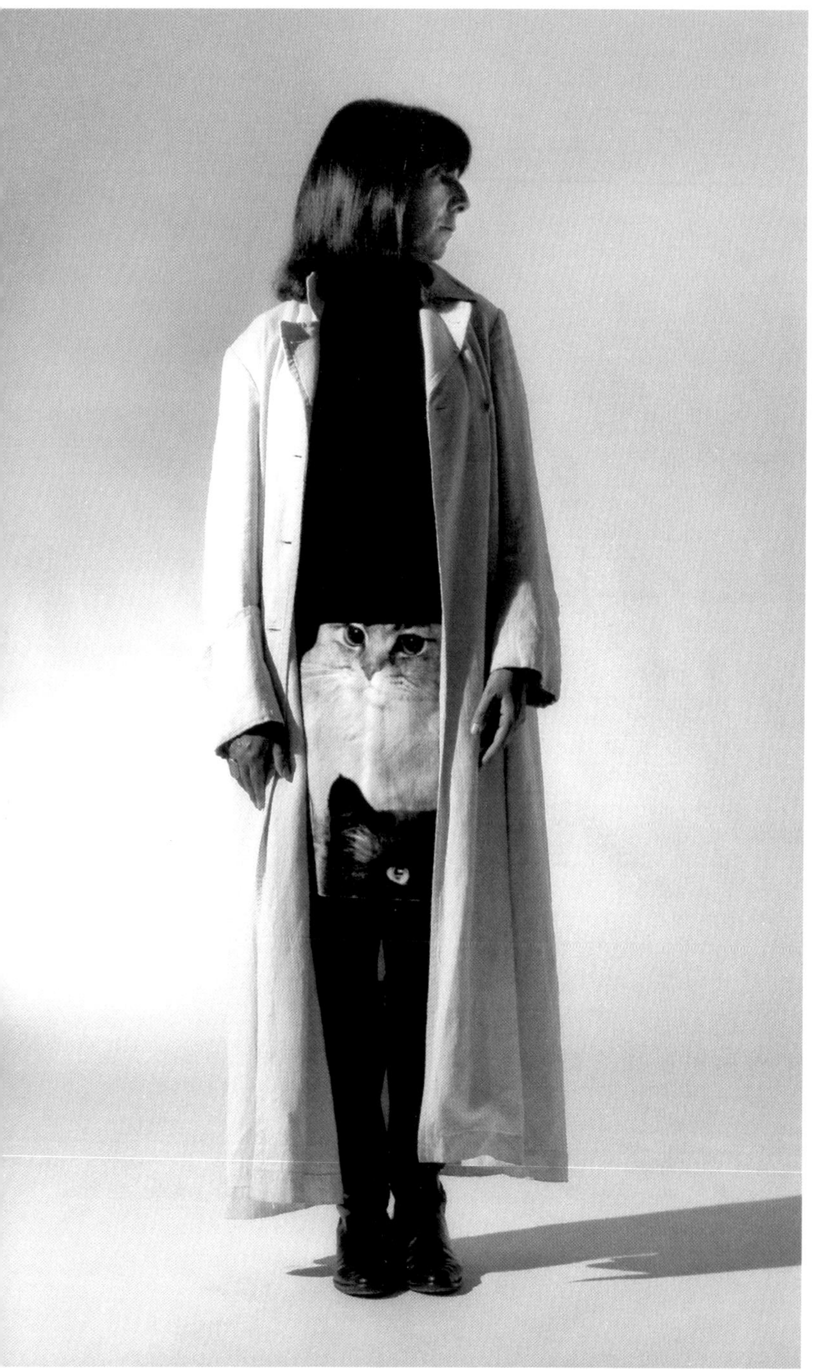

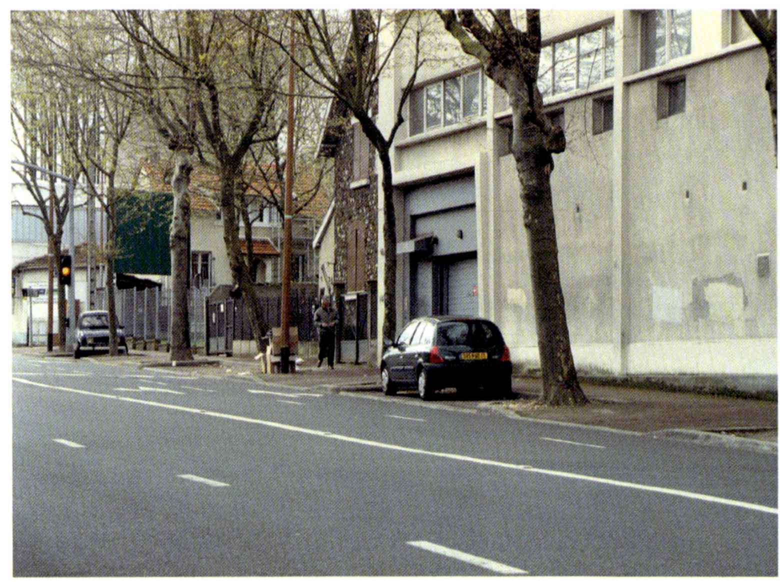

Monday, April 16, 2001.
9:30 a.m. Set out.

At 9:55 I am in position near the building at 146 Boulevard Camélinat, in MALAKOFF (92), the home of Madame Sophie CALLE. It is an old factory or workshop that has been transformed into a loft-style apartment.

The name CALLE is clearly visible on the intercom.

The white AUTOBIANCHI, number 126 AVY 92, which was mentioned to me beforehand as the vehicle habitually used by Madame Sophie CALLE, is parked in the small lot located under the building.

At 10:35 I see a woman fully matching the description of Madame Sophie CALLE leave the parking lot in the aforementioned vehicle. She stops and walks back to the garage.

I observe that today she is wearing a long white raincoat over a skirt in shades of yellow, that she has on boots and is carrying a beige handbag.

At 10:36 she returns to her vehicle and heads for PARIS via the Porte de Vanves.

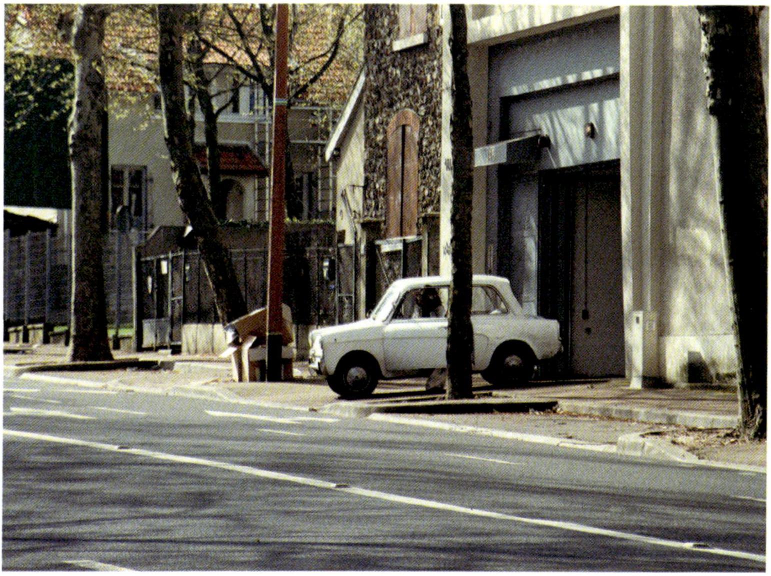

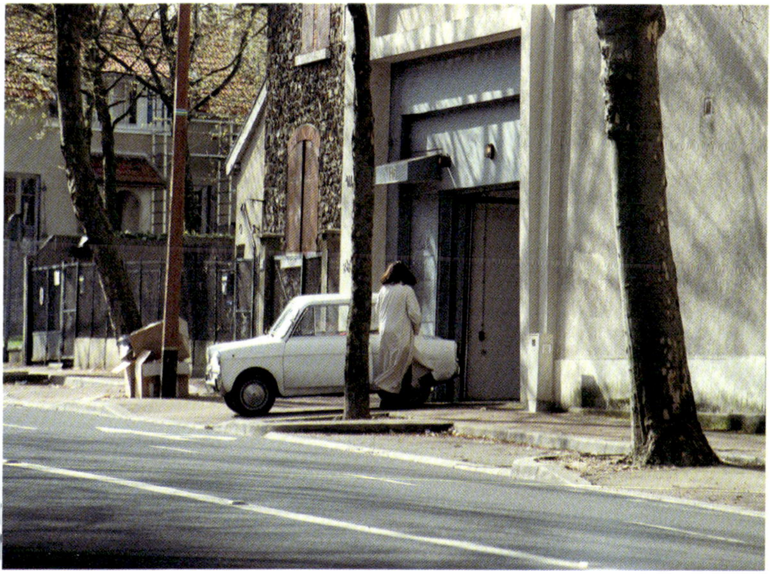

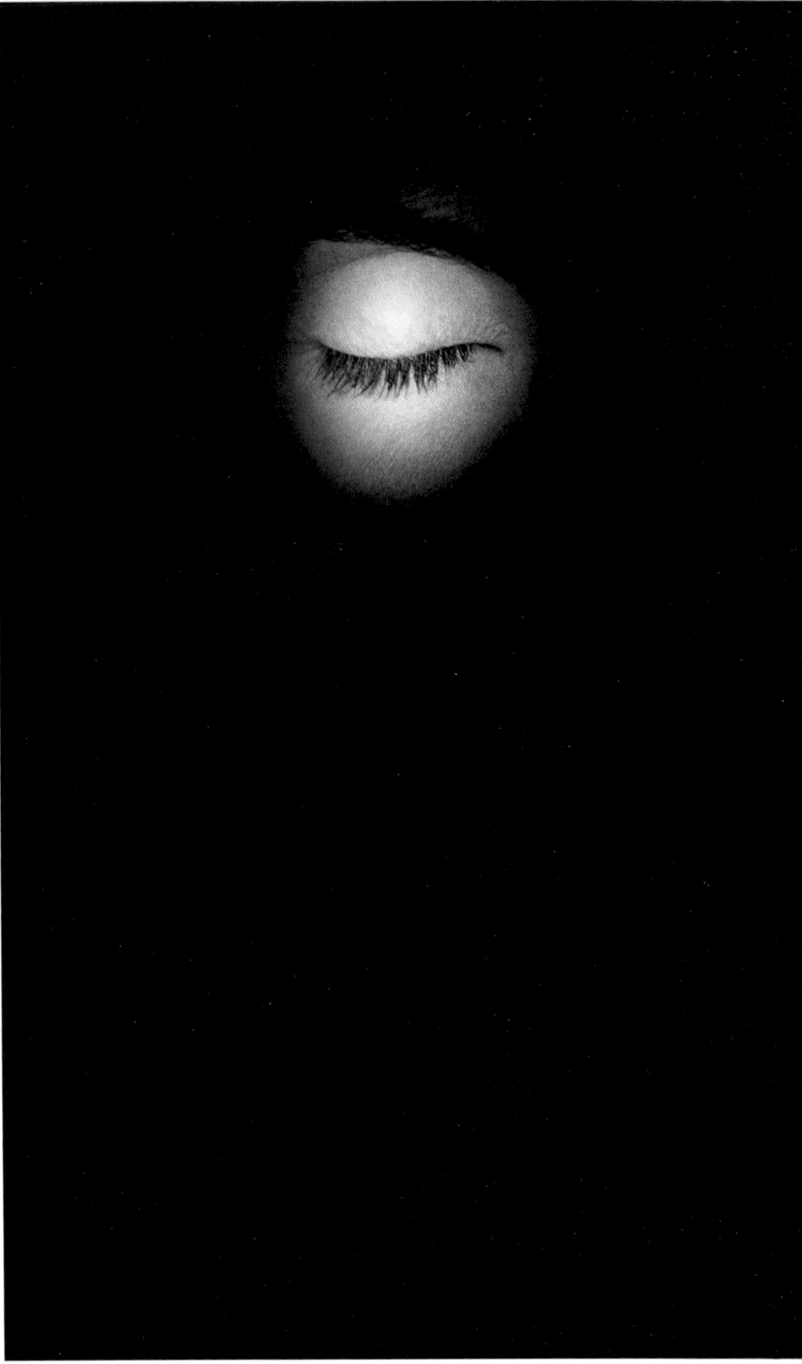

A Certain Gaze

The Blind, 1986
Last Seen, 1991
The Last Image, 2010
Voir la mer, 2011
What do you see?, 2013

The Blind

I met people who were born blind. Who had never seen.
I asked them what their image of beauty was.

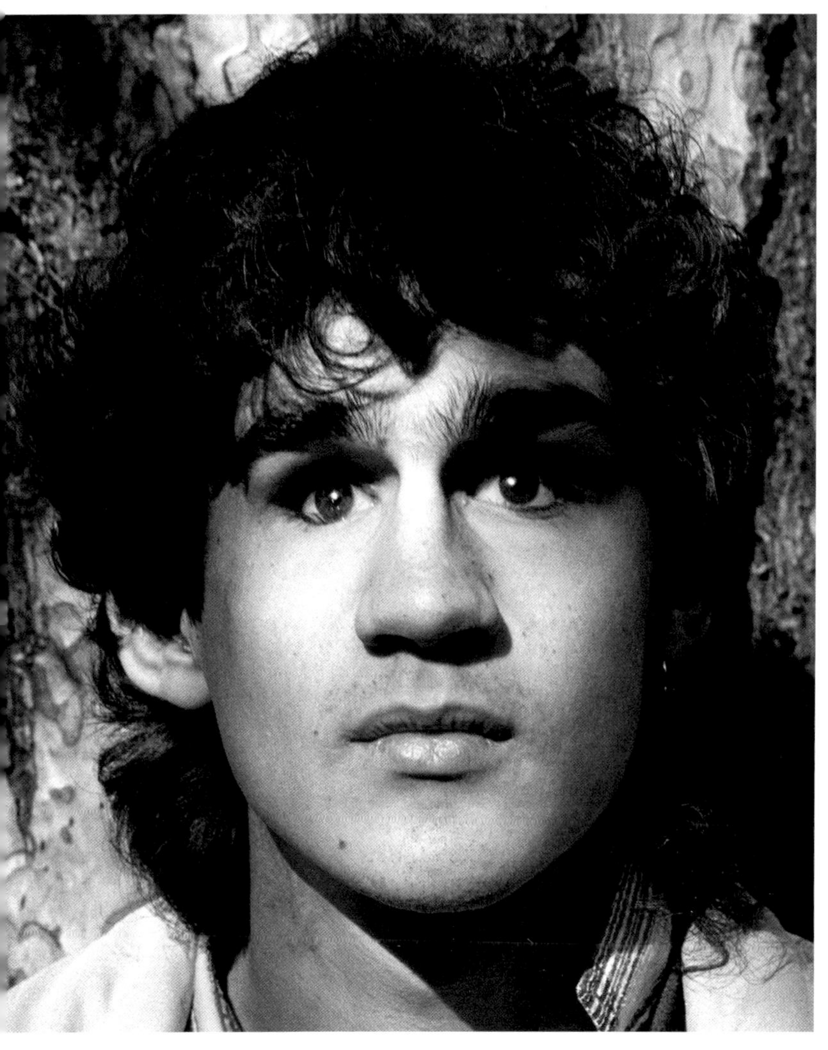

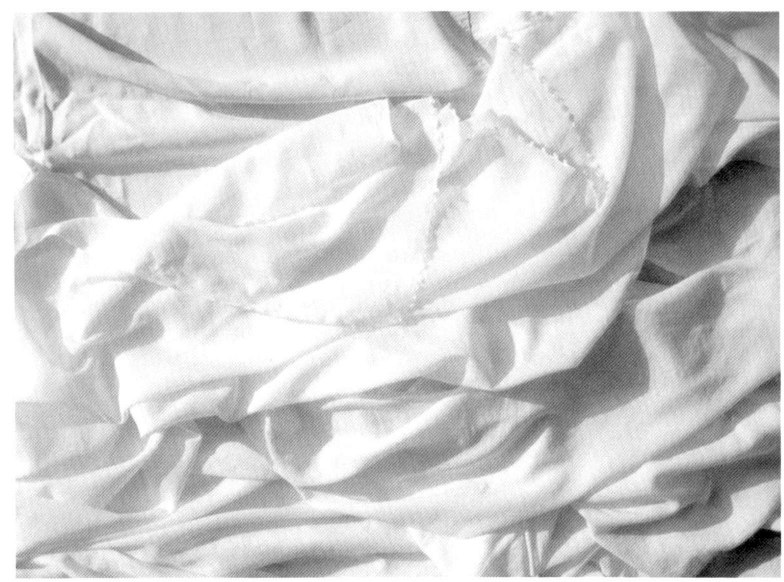

White

White must be the color of purity. I'm told white is beautiful. So I think it's beautiful. But even if it weren't beautiful, it would be the same thing.

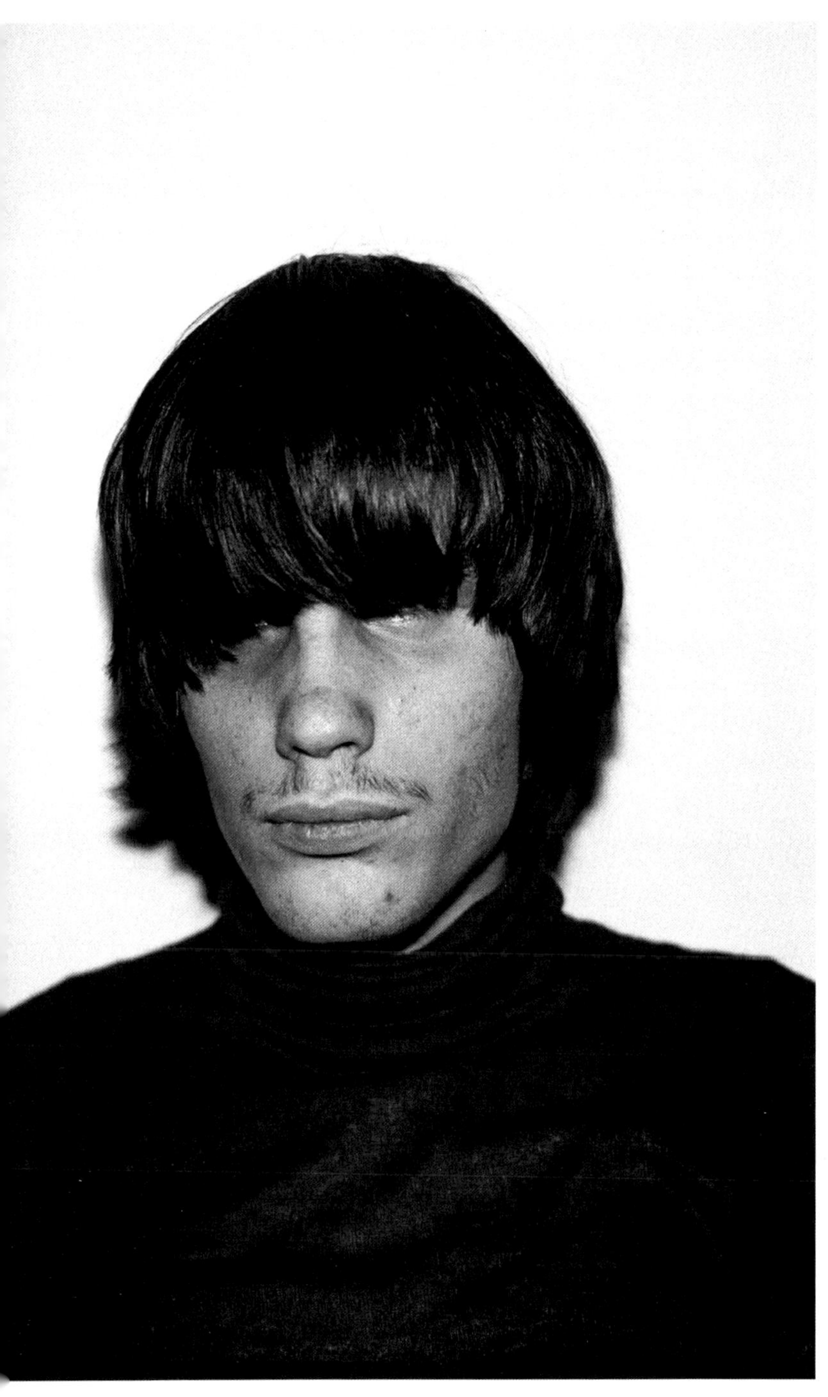

Last Seen

On March 18, 1990, five drawings by Degas, a vase, a Napoleonic eagle, and six paintings by Rembrandt, Flinck, Manet, and Vermeer were stolen from the Isabella Stewart Gardner Museum in Boston. Isabella Stewart Gardner expressly stipulated in her will that nothing in the display should be changed after her death. After the theft, I photographed the empty spaces that the paintings and objects had occupied and I asked the curators, guards, and other staff members to describe their recollection of the missing works.

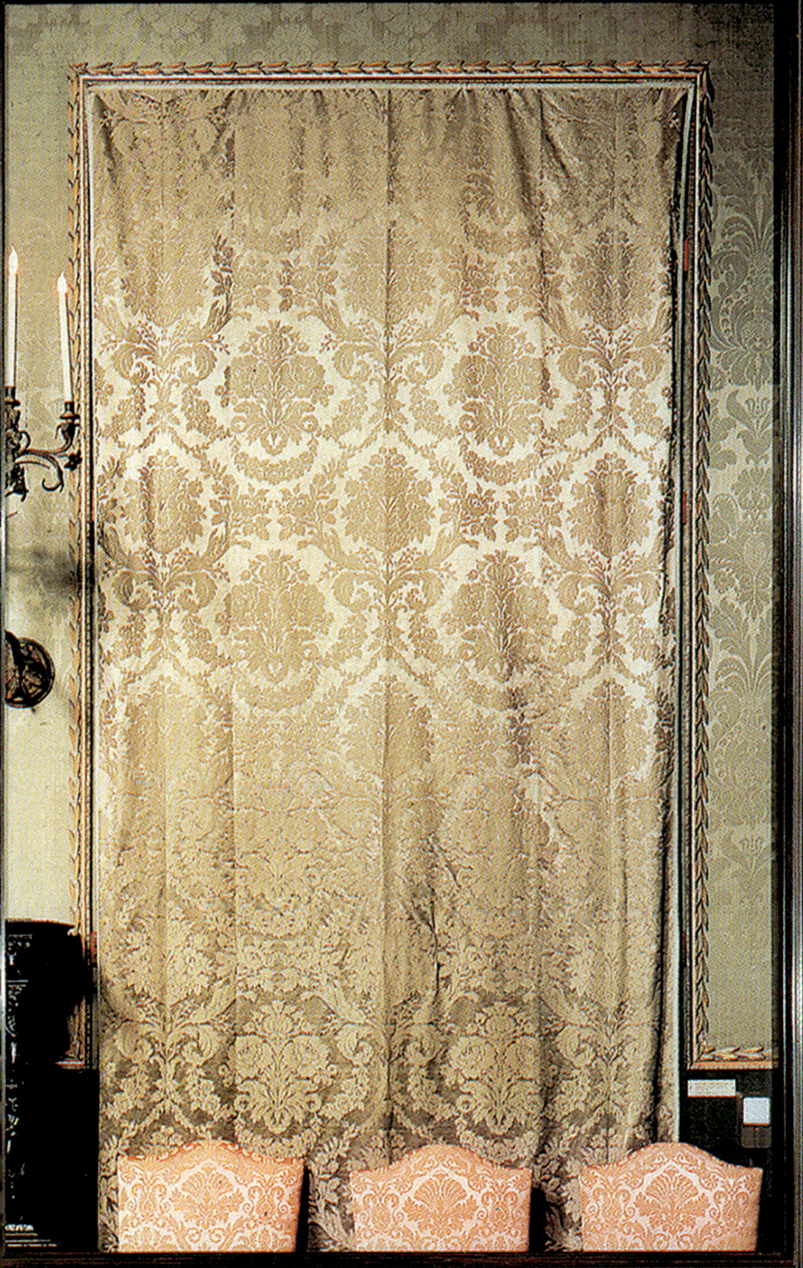

Vermeer, *The Concert*

I'll always remember this painting because I couldn't see it. It was displayed at waist height, behind a chair, covered with glass but next to the window so that the glare caught the glass • I remember there was a painting there but I couldn't describe what was in it. I remember it had a gold frame, very thick, carved, ornate • In the foreground, there was a dark shape, I believe it was a piano, with a large textile, an oriental rug, covering it and an instrument, like a cello, partly tucked under the rug. In the middle ground were the three figures. One was a girl playing the harpsichord and she wore this yellow bodice with puffed sleeves and a white skirt. Then, there was a man playing the lute, with his back to you, sitting in a chair, wearing a red coat, I think. On the right, the woman singing was in blue. She looked pregnant and held her hand just above her swollen belly. There were two paintings hanging in the background. One of them was a wild, dark, savage picture of a forest. The other, just above the head of the singer, was *The Procuress* by Van Baburen. It's a picture of an older woman, who is sort of a pimp, selling this young woman with a lot of cleavage to a distinguished businessman who is looking very salaciously at her, and it's such a rude counterpoint to this very pristine, demure scene of the concert. You had this dark shadowy corner that was somewhat ominous, then this lovely afternoon concert, and then this very lusty, bawdy picture within this very sedate and sensitive one • It's a peaceful thing. I used to look at it every morning before work • I used to come here at night, late at night and just to go up there and stand • There was a woman sitting at the harpsichord. She is so lost in her world of ideas that she's not even present. The other one, who is holding this ethereal scrap of paper, is exquisitely homely. And turning his back to us, sits the mysterious individual, this long-haired gentleman whom we will never know. He plays a guitar-like object and it's almost sort of phallic, especially since this pregnant woman is standing there • It seemed like a very innocent painting although the scholars would say that it had a lot of sexual energy in it. But, I just heard the piano and the woman's voice • The colors that were the most dramatic were the black and the white in the tiled floor but the brightest point was this yellow in the girl's dress. Just sheer yellow paint • The black and white of the floor just jumped at you, but it's the red back of the chair that would catch my attention. This rectangle of red light, in the center of the picture, like a bull's eye • And, of course, there's the lighting. It was just about as good as you can get. The light that came from left to right was just stunning • I thought it was very flat. The colors were muted. You couldn't see the faces of the characters and I was unsure of what was really going on. I don't know if it's because Vermeer was a bad painter or because he intended it to be that way. There was a tremendous sense of intelligence and order in that work. Like a scientific grid. I saw it more as a series of planes. You could almost slice it. The forms were very rounded and yet, the organization was very flat • I can remember its depth. It's Vermeer. You know, Vermeer is Vermeer and it was a Vermeer • The beautiful thing about this Vermeer is that you have silence in a concert. You are looking at such stillness and yet, you know that they're making music • I could hear them singing but it seemed very private, quiet and pure. You felt like an intruder and you wouldn't want them to know you were watching, I didn't like it much, not my style.

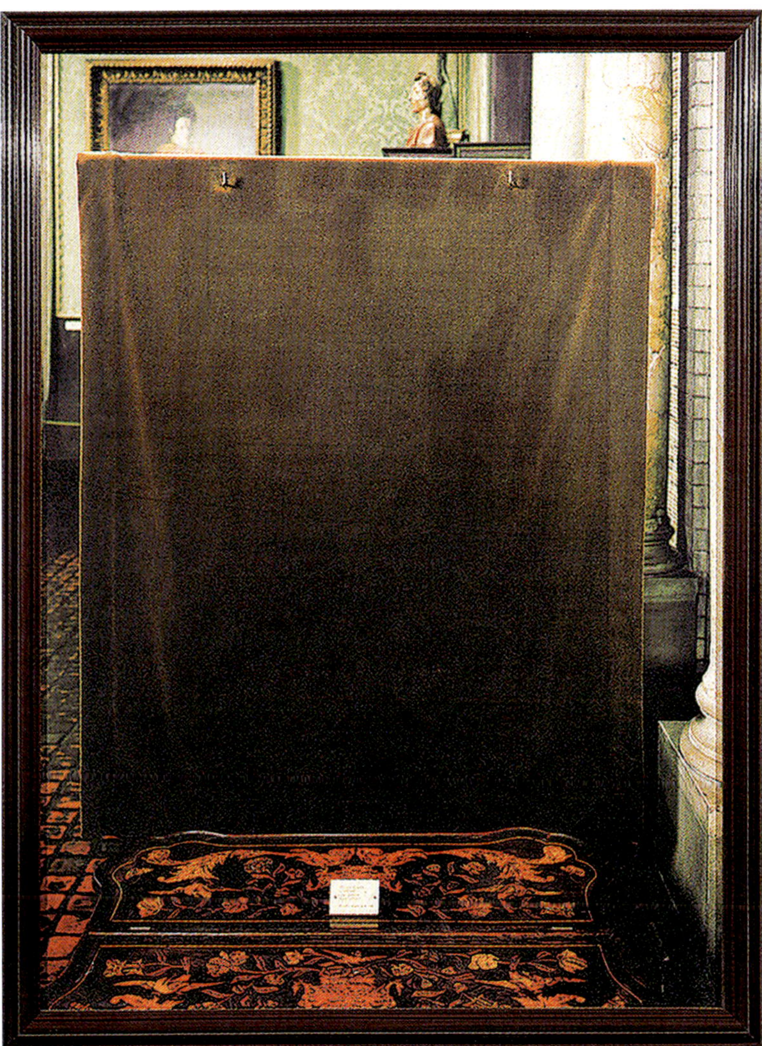

The Last Image

In Istanbul, I met blind people, most of whom had lost their sight suddenly.
I asked them to describe the last thing they saw.

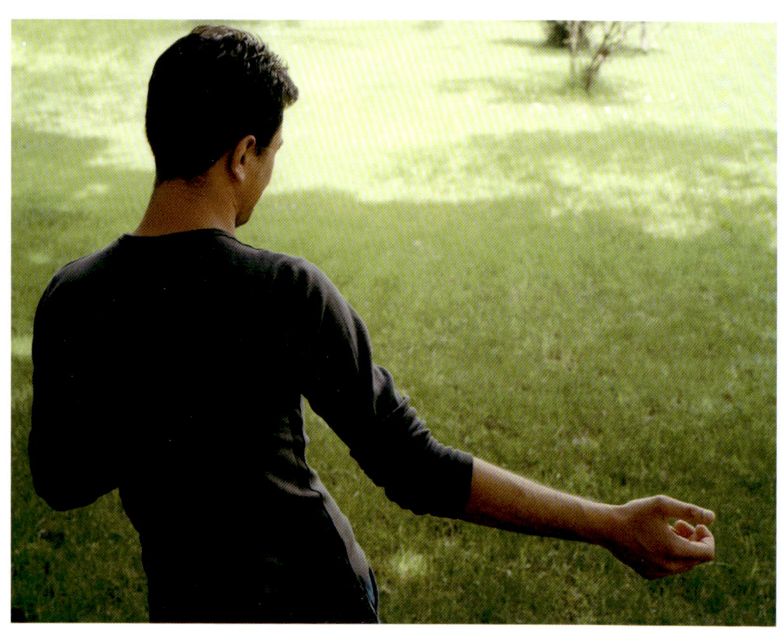

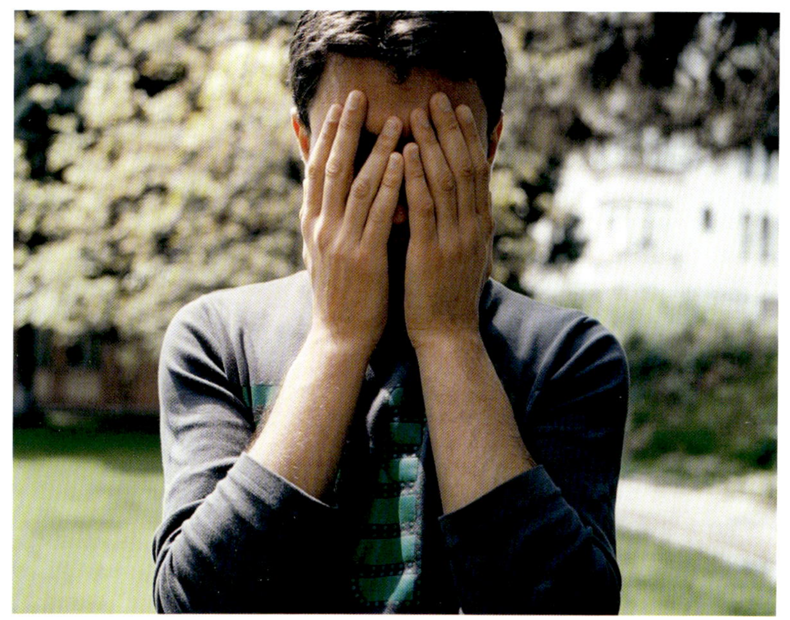

Blind to a Rifle

It was August 5, 1998, at around three in the afternoon. I was minding the cows. In the four corners of the field there was freshly plowed land and, in the center, a garden of green beans. In the distance, the Binbogă Mountains, and above, the scudding clouds. Fifty meters ahead, with his back to me, I saw a hunter dressed in black, aged about twenty-five, his gun pointing slightly downward. A quail flew up in front of the hunter. A dog sprang forward when it saw the bird. The hunter saw the dog. Then he took aim at the bird. The bird flew over the hunter and toward me. The hunter turned slowly. He fired. At the same time, I saw the quail taking flight, the dog springing forward, the hunter's movement. I heard the rifle shot. I covered my eyes.

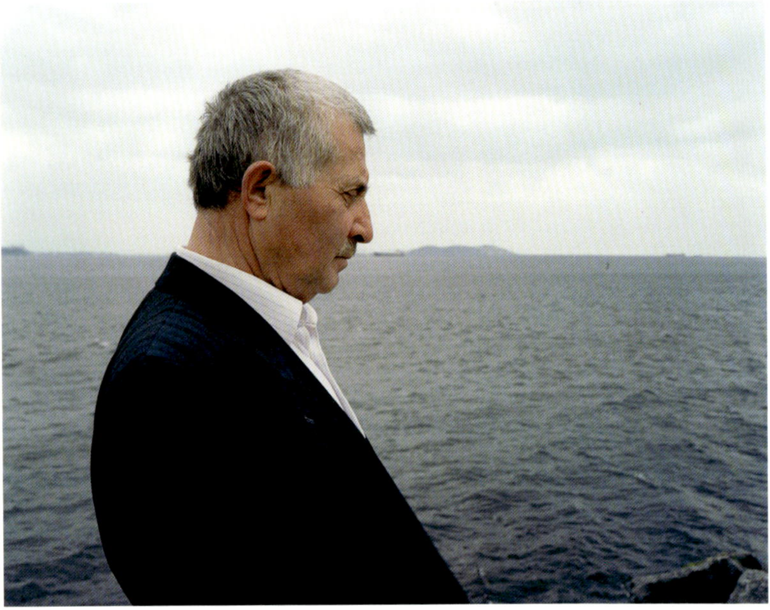

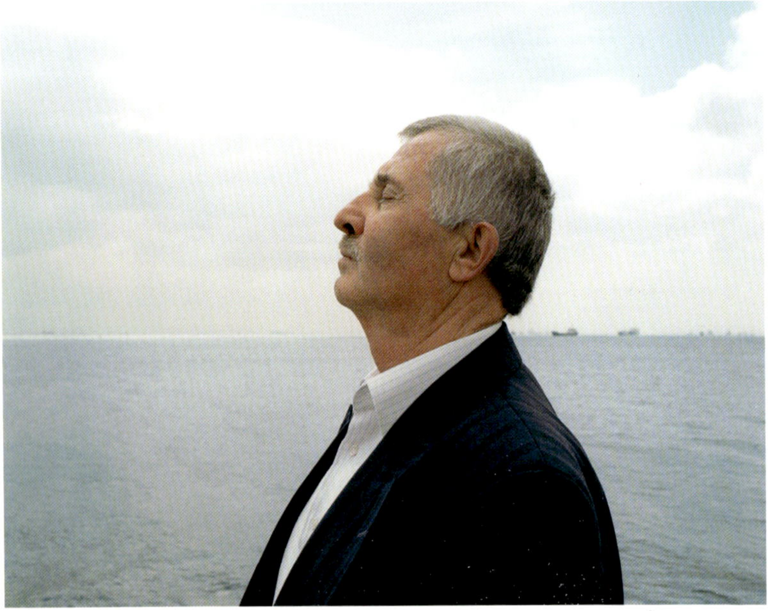

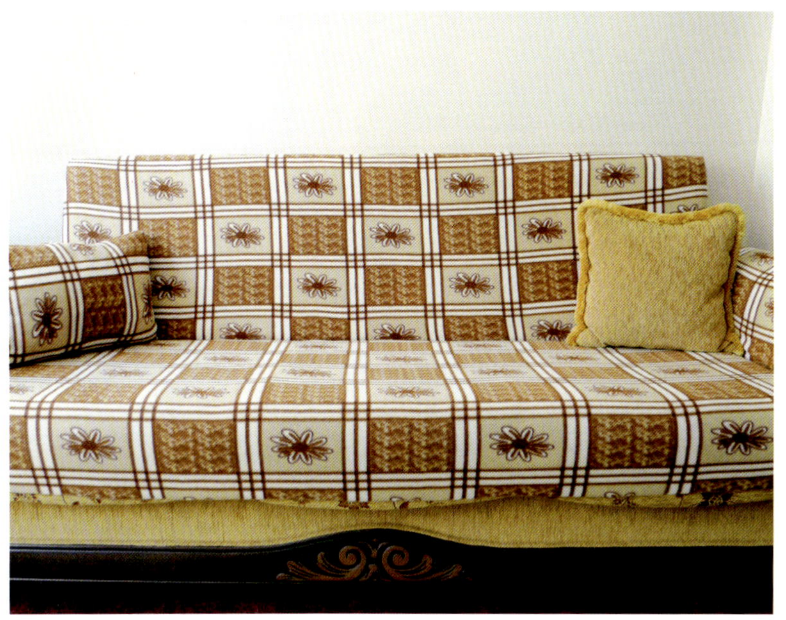

Blind to a Sofa

There is no last image—my loss of eyesight was gradual—but there is an image that remains, the one that's missing: three children that I can't see, sitting side by side, facing me, on the living-room sofa, where you are now.

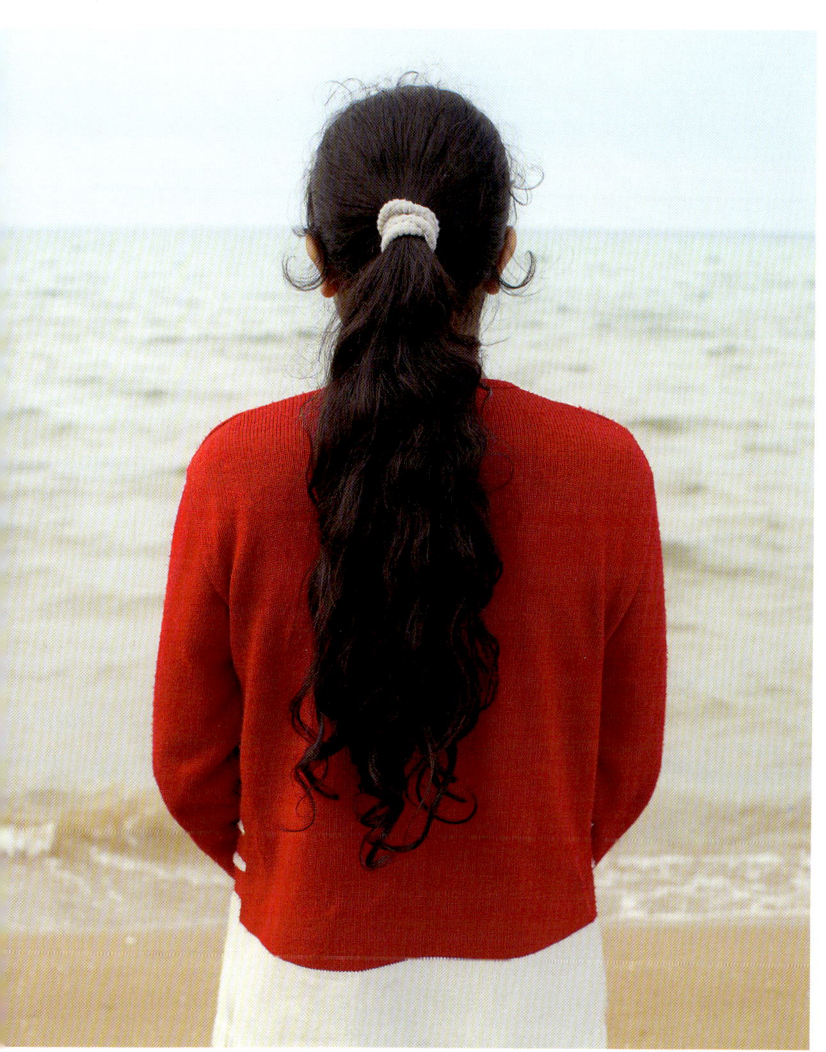

Young Girl in Red

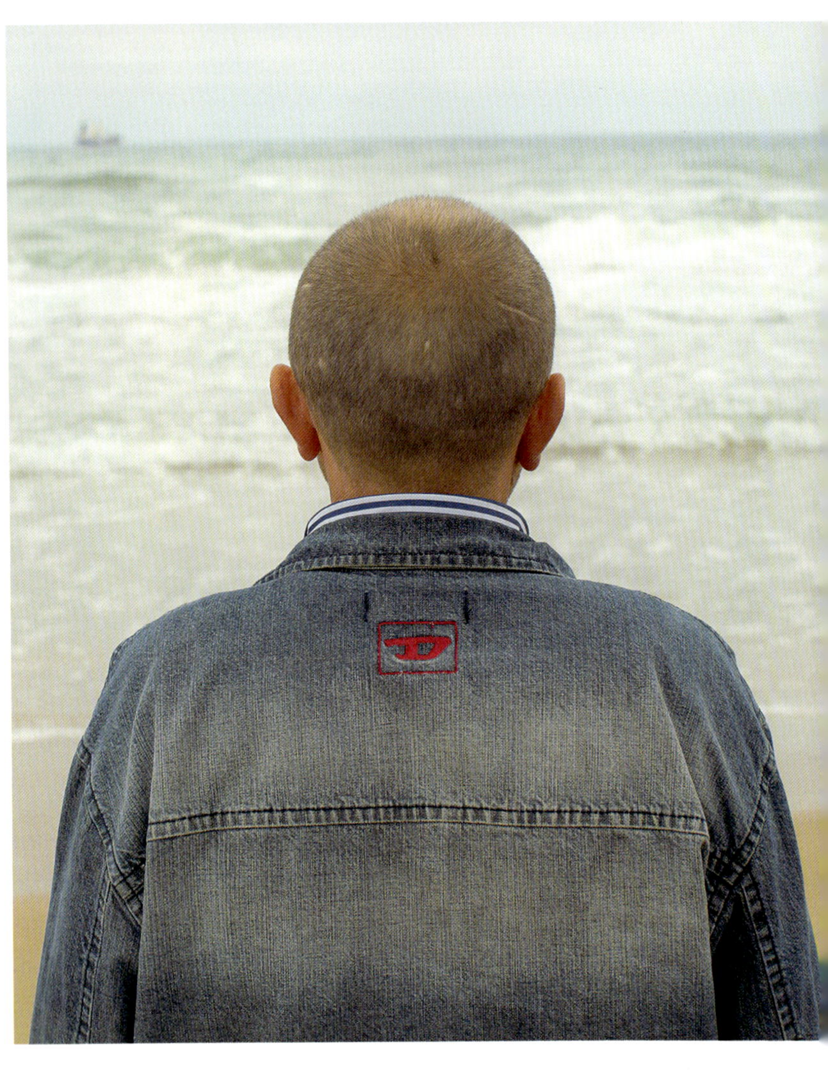

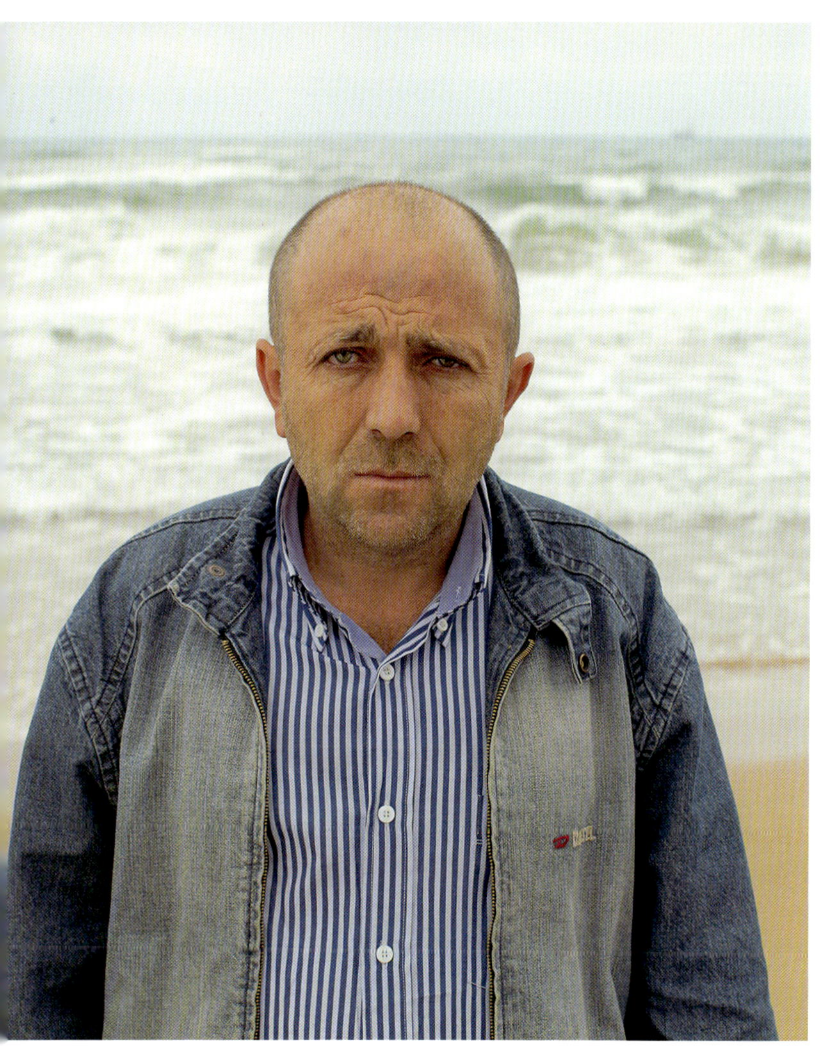

Deep Man

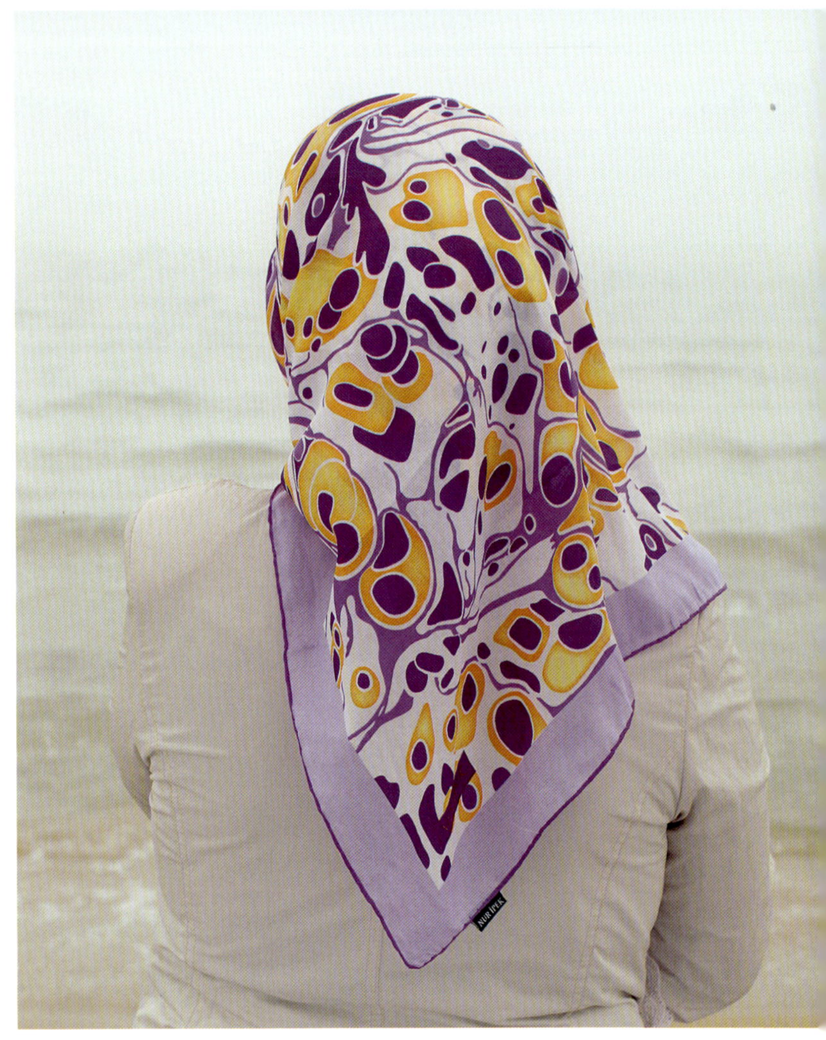

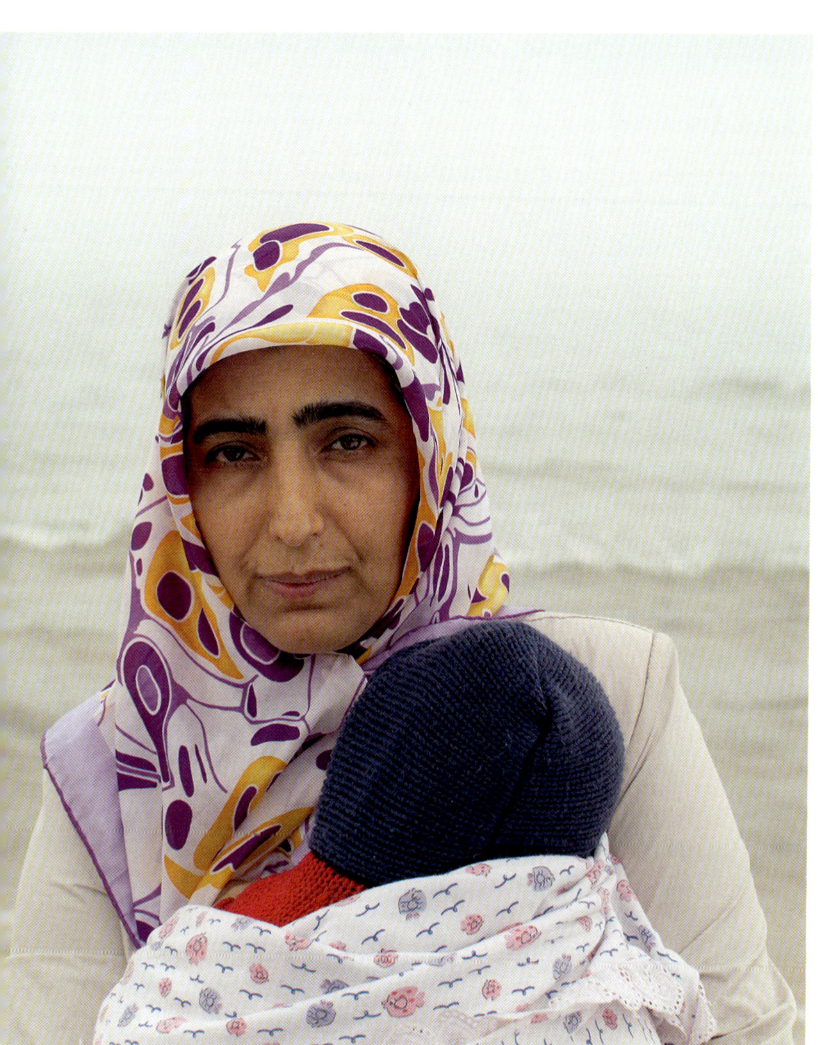

Woman with Baby

What do you see?

On March 18, 1990, after the theft of artworks from the Isabella Stewart Gardner Museum in Boston, the frames of paintings by Vermeer, Flinck and Rembrandt were left behind. These were then restored and put back in position, further emphasizing the absence of the works. I asked the curators, guards, other staff members and visitors to tell me what they saw within these frames.

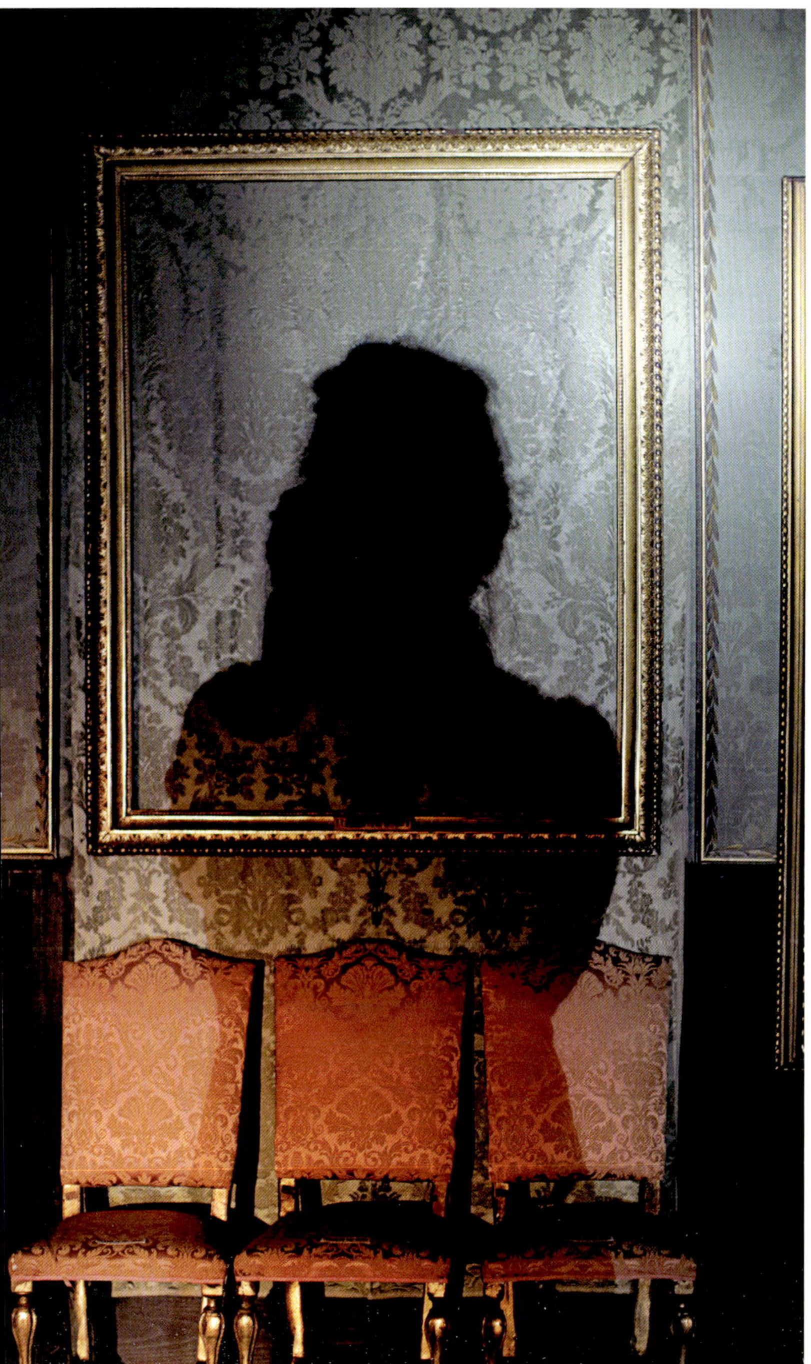

Vermeer, *The Concert*
When I stand in front of this empty space, I see a woman deep in concentration
playing the harpsichord, and the woman on the other side just about to emit a
note from her body. And I hear music playing • I see a very old wooden frame with
no picture in it, and behind it, a brown background, a velvet cloth. That's all there
is. There's no reason for this frame to be here. What am I supposed to see? This
empty space represents space, just space • The picture arises. I contemplate
a painting stronger than its absence. If you know this work, you see it better in
the velvet than in a reproduction. I see people making music. You are looking at
this silent picture but you're aware of music being made in the painting. A lute
player with his back to you, a woman at a harpsichord and a woman singing,
palpable. In my dreams I mostly see her. I am so attached to her that I should be
able to know where she is • I don't see much of anything. I see an empty frame,
and behind the frame is this very dark fabric. I certainly see a solemn space.
A little bit reproachful • I see colors. On the left, the yellow sleeve of the woman,
the trapezoidal red shape of the back of the chair and then that blue ... I see the
luxurious jacket the singer is wearing and the shadowy foreground with that rich,
oriental carpet over the table. I see three colors, that sort of dance across the
surface. It's red, yellow, blue—it's Mondrian • I see flashes of what is supposed
to be there. I see *The Concert*. When I give people a tour, I point and I say: this is
The Concert. But there is nothing there. Except a framed space that represents
frustration • I see a black fabric, a little bit spooky. It says I could put anything I
wanted inside the frame, but the blackness seems to be fighting against my desire
to imagine something in there • I've never seen this picture in person, so I see
crime-scene pictures. The frame lying on the floor, in the middle of the room, with
broken glass contained within. The chalk line they put around the body—that's
what this frame is to me. But it never goes away; you see the body every day • It's a
sad and nostalgic image. I see textures and nuances. I see this soft light washing
over the velvet. I see this dark shadow to the right, and this very pale horizontal
line across the center. I see this tiny layer of dust, especially on the lower left-hand
edge. And of course, because the velvet is so spare and simple, I focus on the
frame, the gold-etched outlines of flowers and the larger floral shapes, almost like
sunflowers, around the edges. The outside is very charged and the inside very
quiet. And, for whatever reason, I have this slight feeling that the frame is looking
at me • I see a frame that shows an absence. I see something everyone is denied
the pleasure of seeing. I see a loss that is just indescribable. I see my impossibility
to ever see the real thing • Today I just see velvet, but of course there's much
more • My job is to bring it back, so I see my failure. I see this void even in my
nightmares. There is a car, and, in it, a painting with a plastic bag over it. I take the
bag off and it's not the painting that I want. But I know that one day, in the middle
of the night, I'll receive a telephone call: *Vermeer is back*.

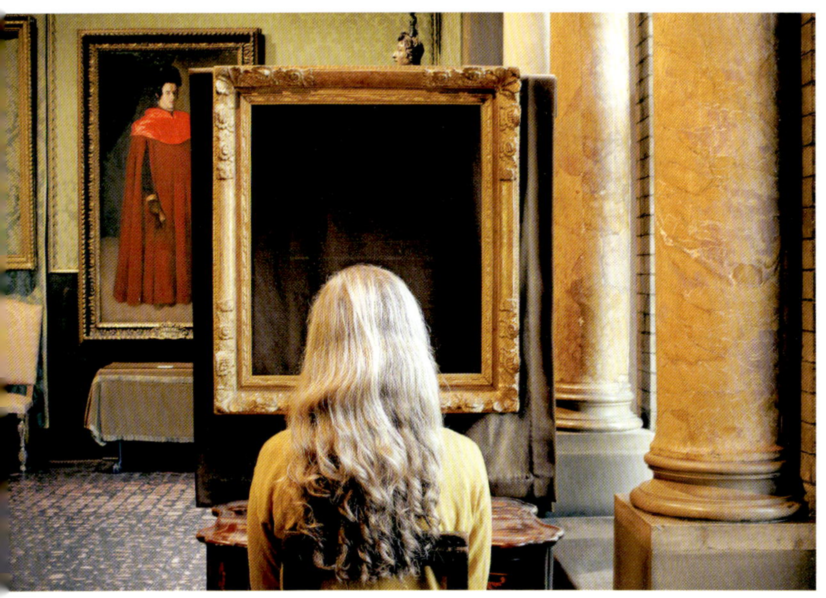

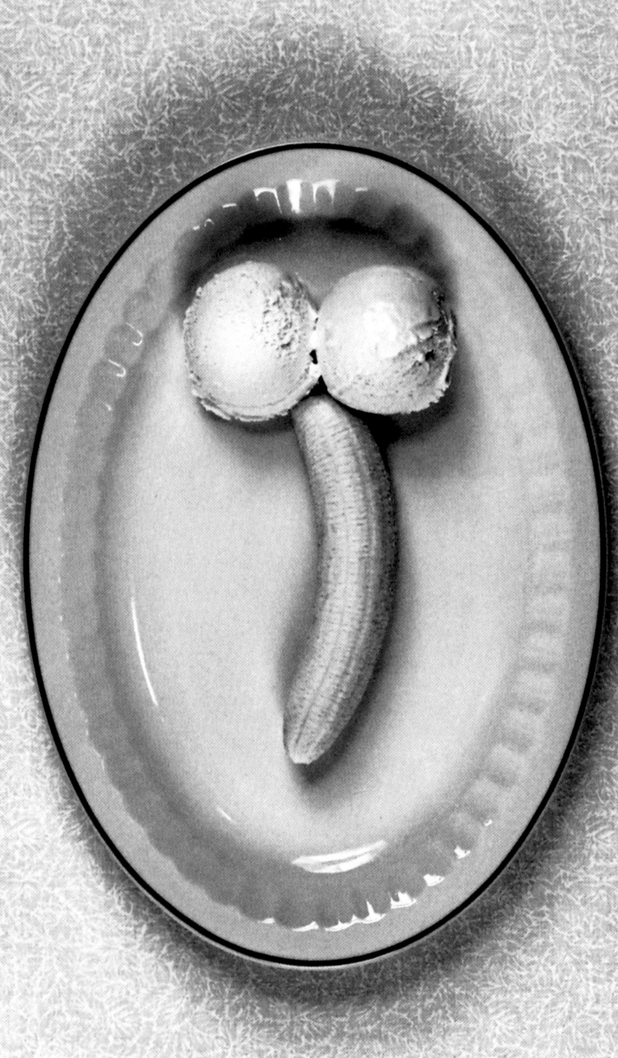

Love Stories

Exquisite Pain, 1984–2003
Take Care of Yourself, 2004–2007
On the Hunt, 2017–2020

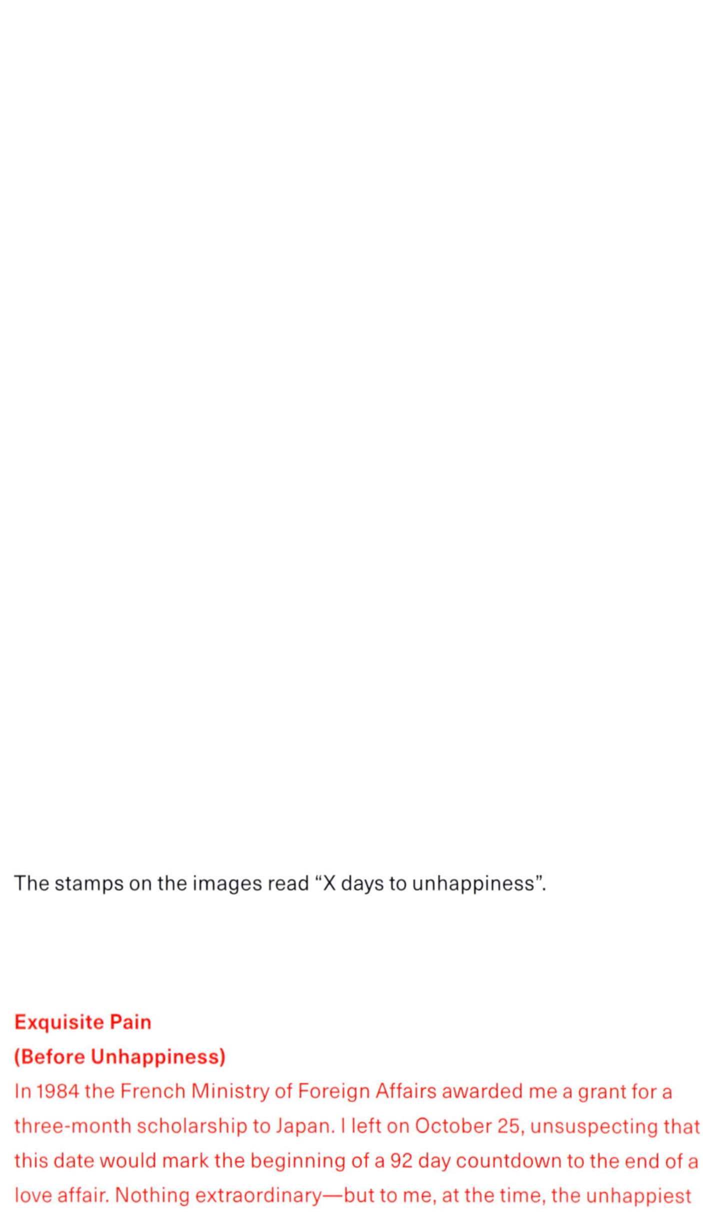

The stamps on the images read "X days to unhappiness".

Exquisite Pain
(Before Unhappiness)
In 1984 the French Ministry of Foreign Affairs awarded me a grant for a three-month scholarship to Japan. I left on October 25, unsuspecting that this date would mark the beginning of a 92 day countdown to the end of a love affair. Nothing extraordinary—but to me, at the time, the unhappiest moment in my life, and one for which I blamed the trip itself.

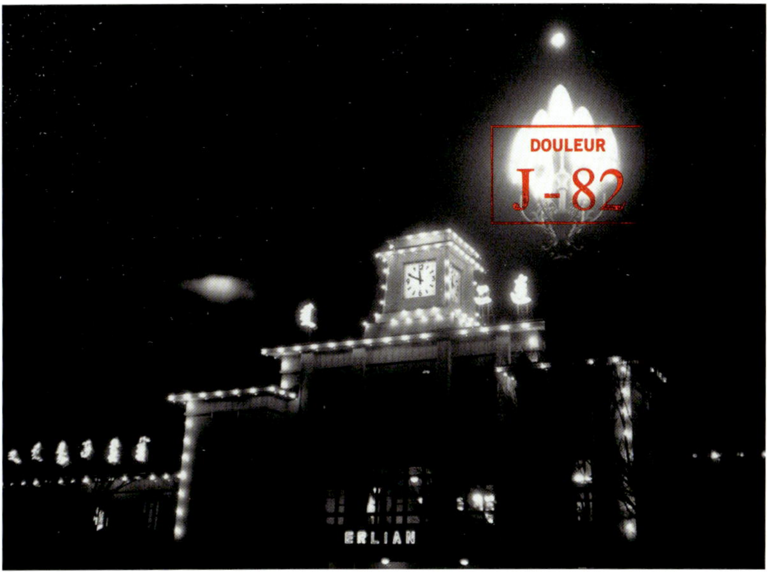

DOULEUR
J-82
ERLIAN

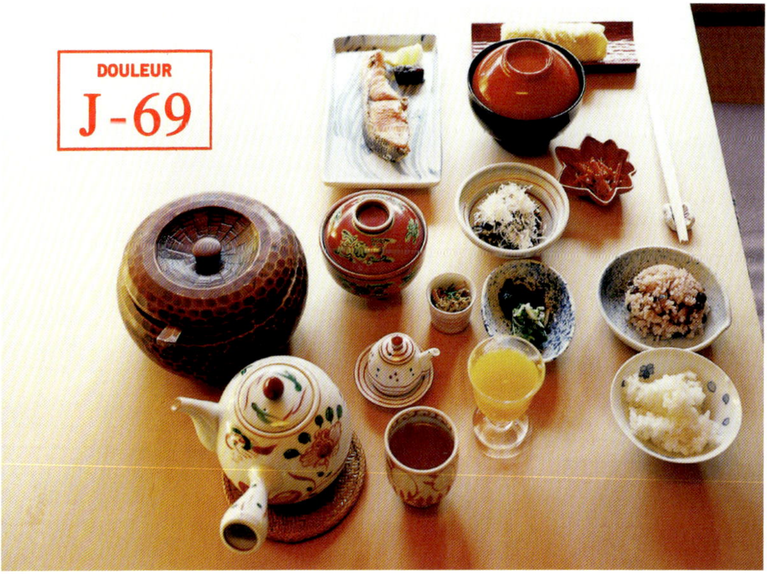

DOULEUR
J-69

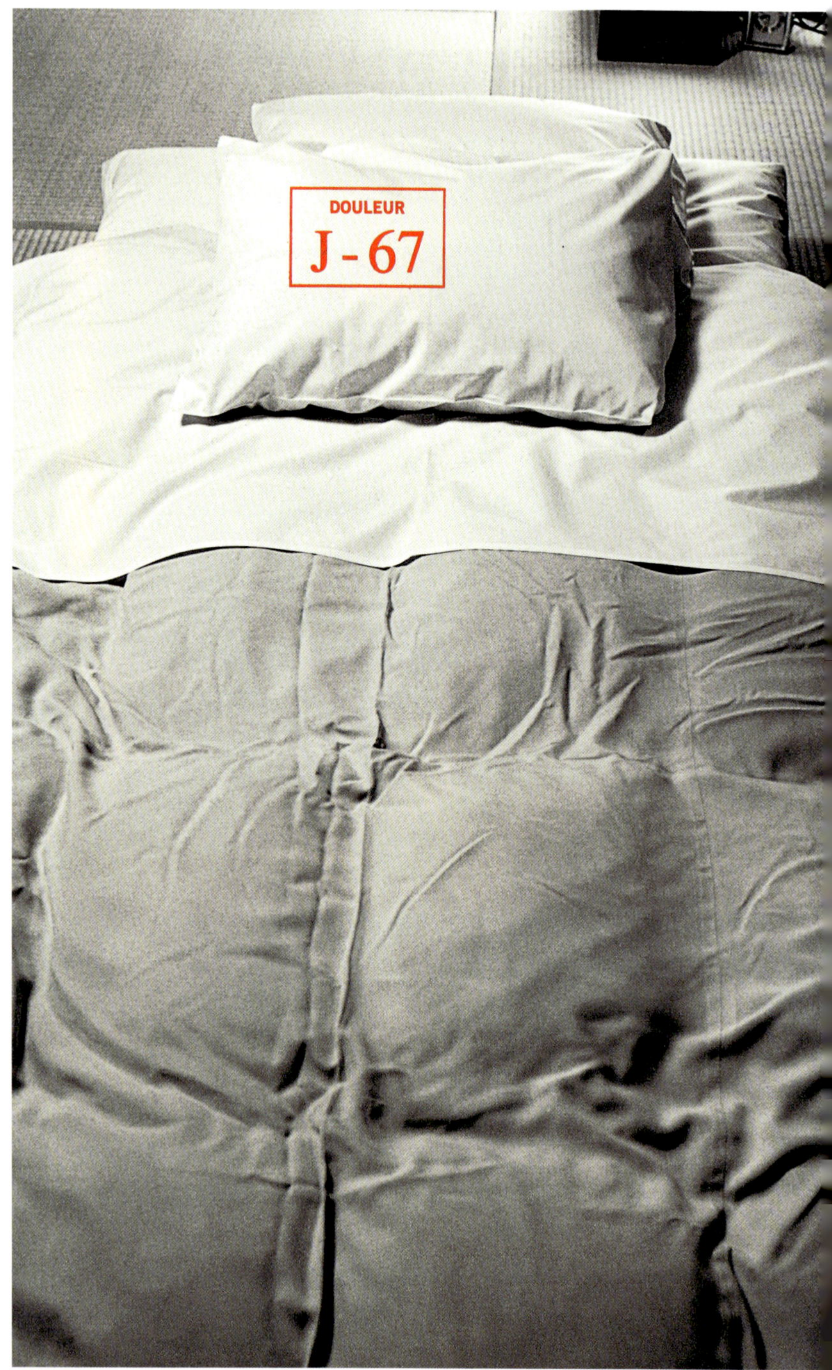
DOULEUR
J-67

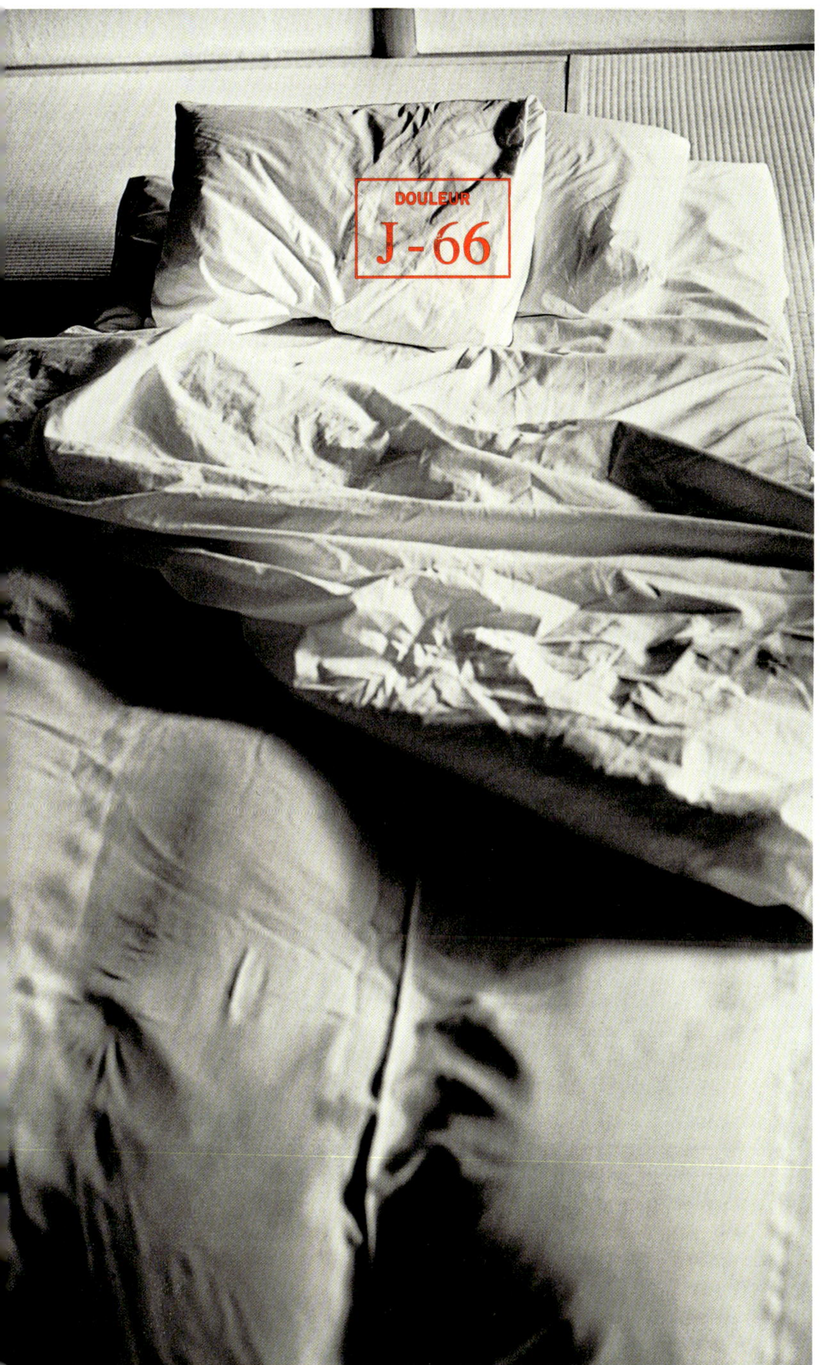
DOULEUR
J - 66

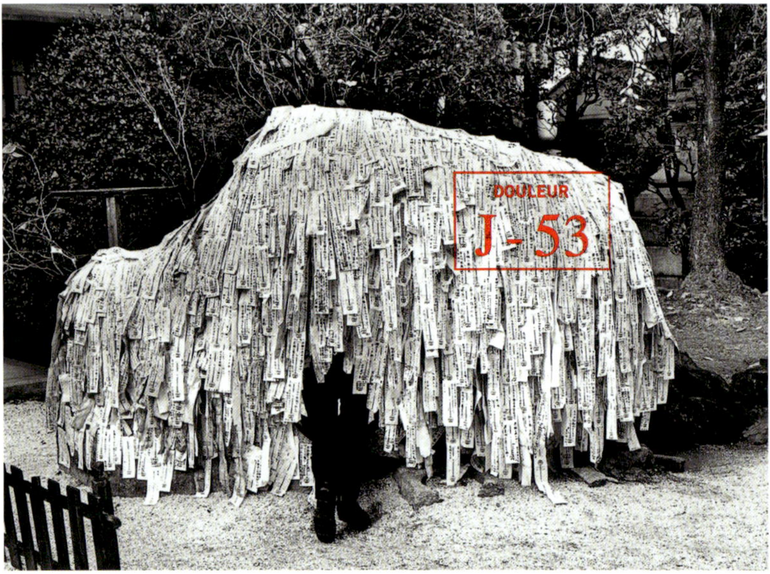

DOULEUR
J - 53

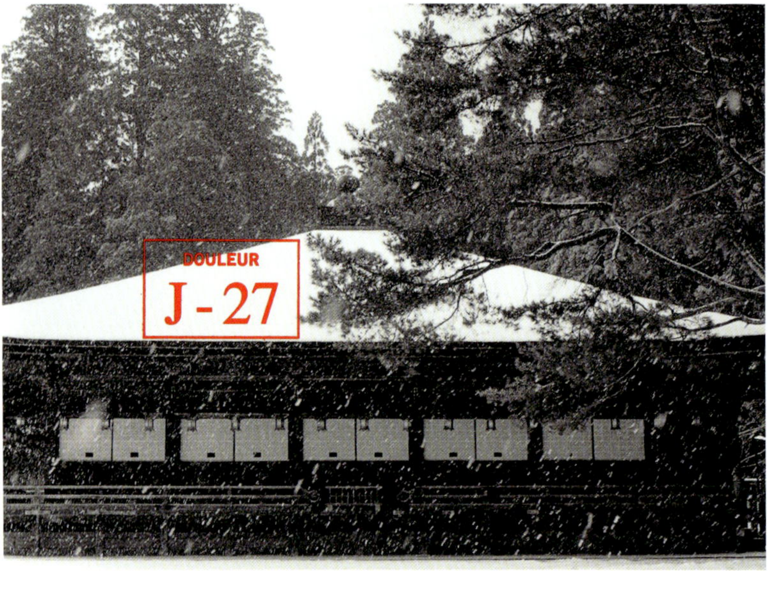

DOULEUR
J - 27

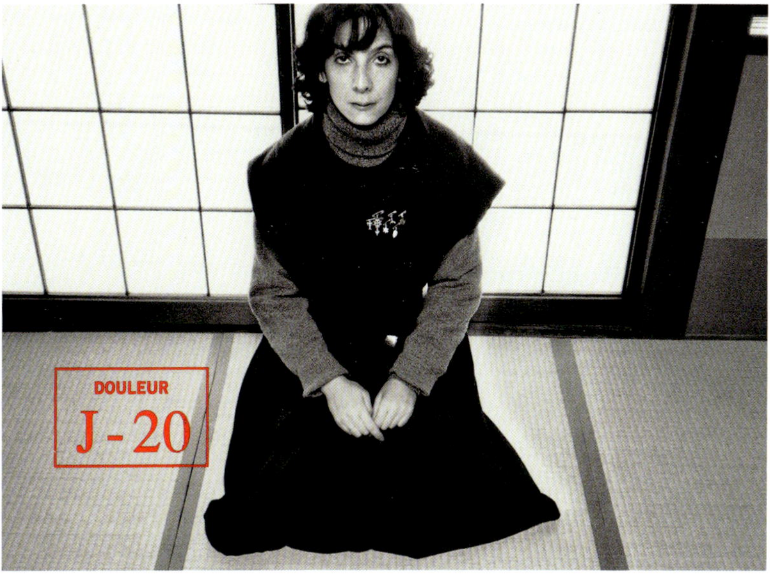

DOULEUR
J - 20

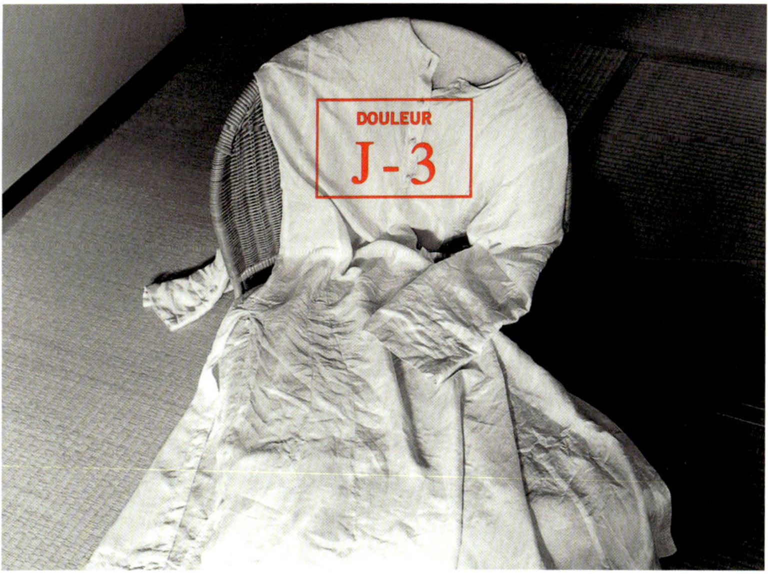

DOULEUR
J - 3

Message from ____________________

Date and Time received __________

WE GOT THE MESSAGE AS FOLLOW.

DOULEUR
J-1

can't join you in DELHI

DUE ACCIDENT IN PARIS and stay in

hospital. PLEASE CONTACT BOB

in paris.

— Thank you —

日本航空 JAPAN AIR LINES

Exquisite Pain

(After Unhappiness)

I got back to France on January 28, 1985. From that moment, whenever people asked me about the trip, I chose to skip the Far East bit and tell them about my suffering instead. In return I started asking both friends and chance encounters: "When did you suffer most?" I decided to continue such exchanges until I had got over my pain by comparing it with other people's, or had worn out my story through sheer repetition. The method proved radically effective. In three months I had cured myself. Yet, while the exorcism had worked, I still feared a possible relapse, and so I decided not to exploit this experiment artistically. By the time I returned to it, fifteen years had passed.

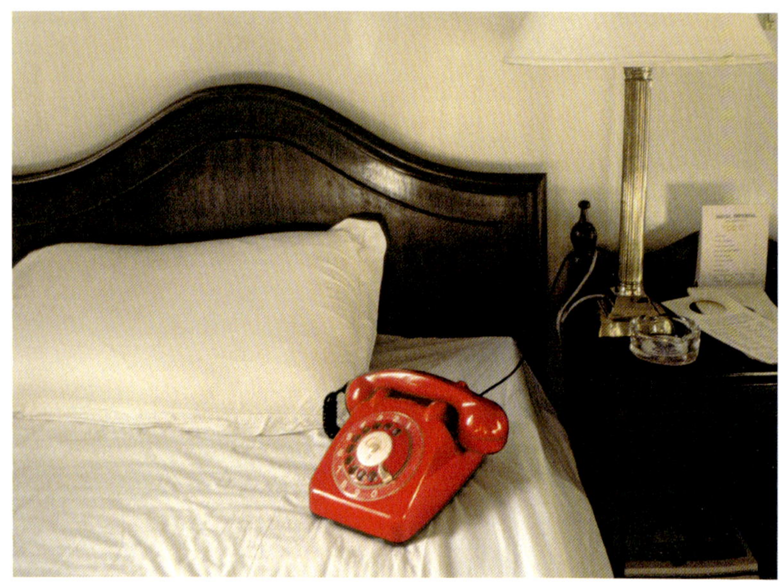

5 days ago, the man I love left me.
He was a friend of my father's. I'd always had a thing for him. On our first
night, I slipped into bed in a wedding dress. Before that day, I had applied
for a three-month study grant for Japan. Unfortunately, the answer was
positive. M. didn't approve of such a long absence. He threatened to forget
me. Maybe I wanted to know if he loved me enough to be patient. Anyway,
I went. For his part, he was going to try and wait. He suggested we meet up
in India after my trip. I left Paris on October 25, 1984. A nightmare. I hated
the whole thing. All I could think about was our reunion, set for January 24.
On the 23rd, three hours before his plane took off, he phoned to confirm
his arrival time: he would be landing before me and would wait in New
Delhi for the plane from Tokyo. I had won. But at the airport they handed
me this message: "M. can't join you in Delhi due accident in Paris and
stay in hospital. Please contact Bob." We had just spoken, so I imagined
an accident on the way to Orly airport. Since Bob, my father, is a doctor,
I pictured M. seriously wounded, maybe even dead. I took the room he'd
reserved at the Imperial Hotel. Impossible to get a connection. It took me
ten hours to get through to my father, who couldn't make head or tail of the
telegram. Yes, M. had been in the hospital but only for ten minutes, to have
an infected finger treated. That was all. I called him at home. He picked
up the phone and he said: "I wanted to come and explain a few things to
you." I replied: "Have you met someone?" "Yes." I spent the rest of the night
staring at the phone. I'd never been this unhappy before.

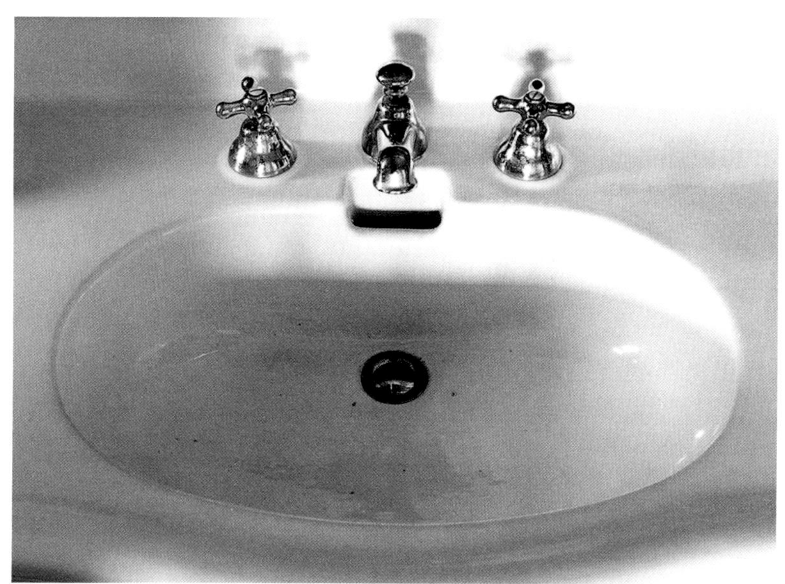

His name was Jean. I was twenty-seven, he was forty-seven. We were
living together. It was real passion, pure passion. That morning, when
I woke up and went to the bathroom, there was a letter on the basin. A few
complicated words. I don't remember what, exactly, but they meant we had
to break up. I had no idea this would happen. I put the letter in my pocket.
I went downstairs. I fled, left everything. I totally blanked out. I was in
analysis. I crossed the Luxembourg Gardens to go to my session. I asked
my analyst to lend me a book so that I could leave with something in my
hands to fill that void. He took from his bookcase an old volume bound in
red Morocco leather, with engravings. Like a sleepwalker, I withdrew from
the world for months. I suffered night and day. I didn't cry, but tears were
constantly streaming from my eyes. And the washbasin obsessed me.
The brutality of the white letter on the washbasin. Perhaps that is why for
the last twelve years I have had an apartment with no bathroom, no basin.

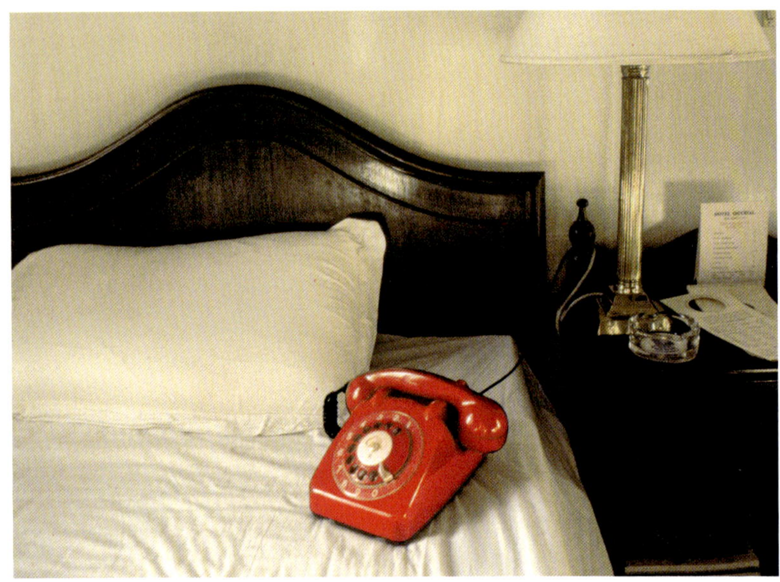

38 days ago, the man I love left me.

We were supposed to be landing together in New Delhi on January 24, 1985. He was coming from Paris, me from Tokyo. I had been gone three months, and the thought of this day was the only thing that kept me going. Except that he wasn't at the airport. Instead of our reunion there was a message telling me he'd been hospitalized after an accident. At two in the morning, sick with worry, as a last resort, I dialed his number. To my surprise, he picked up the phone. He had indeed been in hospital for an infected finger. That's how I found out he had met another woman and was leaving me. All this in only three minutes. I hung up. An infection of the finger. Caused by a splinter. That would be me. An infected finger... Incredible. Also called a whitlow. Funny. But I wasn't amused, not yet. Heartbroken, stunned. I spent the rest of the night in that room 261 of the Imperial Hotel with my eyes on the red telephone.

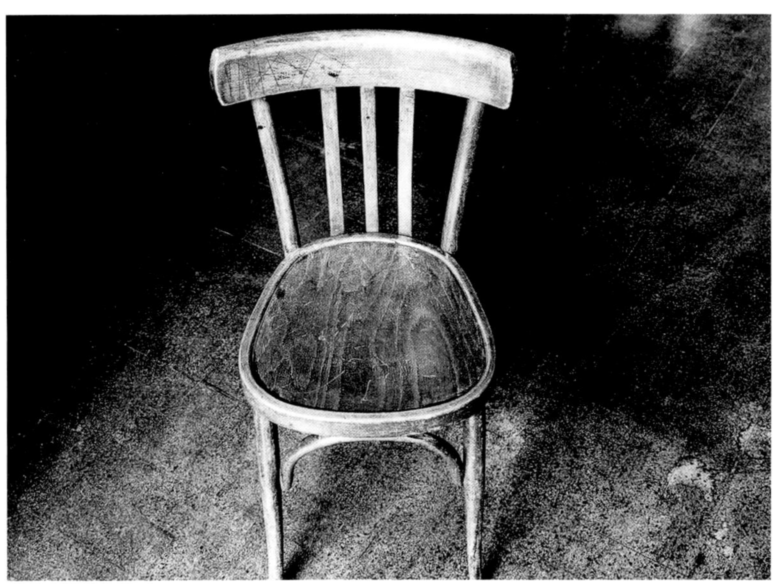

I spent a whole summer sitting on a chair, at home in Paris. In 1972. Suffering with no apparent cause. Three months in that chair, doing nothing. Stiff, still, eyes open, hands on knees—I stayed in that position for ten hours a day. I have no recollection of the nights. The only visit I remember is the light that came into the room— a dilapidated room, about forty square meters—at around twelve-thirty p.m. and left at about seven p.m. The phone had been cut off. There was no music. The chair was uncomfortable. Why that chair? Because it forced me to keep a certain posture. On a bed, I would have died.

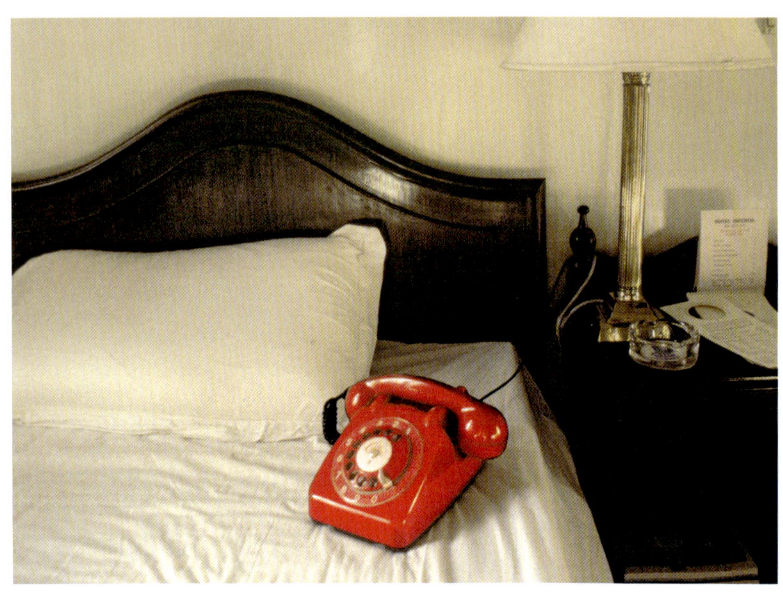

98 days ago, the man I love left me.

January 25, 1985. Room 261. Imperial Hotel. New Delhi. *Enough.*

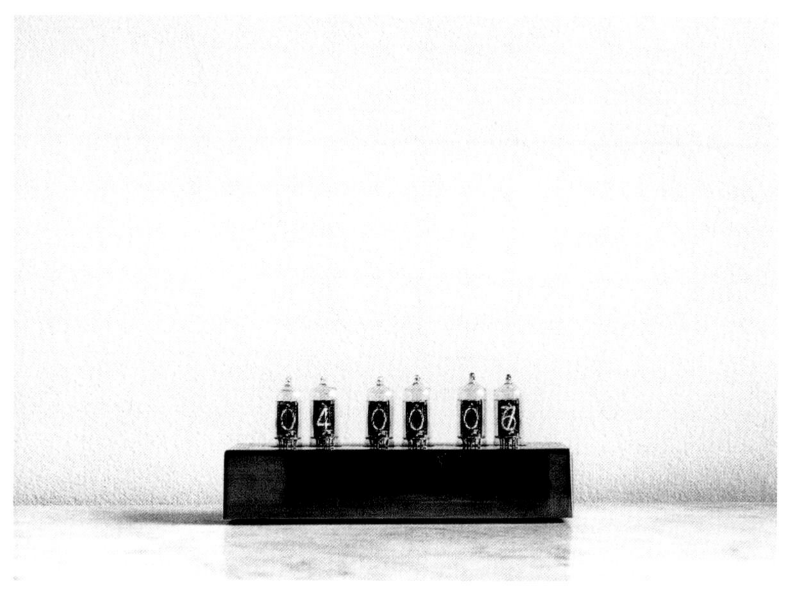

The setting is a village in northern Italy. My parents are out. Suddenly, in the night, we hear a cart, voices. My mother comes in. She says my father isn't well. I look at the face of this man who, two hours ago, was my father, as he lies there, not moving. I hear my mother giving orders. She tells my brother to go fetch some ice. She sends me out for the priest. Everything is speeded up. In the bedroom there is the doctor, the priest, my brother, my mother. I keep my eyes on her. She is my guide. She seems extremely calm. The doctor says the children should leave the room. She refuses: "I want my children to see their father die." Time goes by, watching this snoring man. The dramatic intensity slowly wanes, replaced by fatigue and a stiff back. I wonder when it will end. He died at exactly four o'clock. When the deep silence settled, my mother opened the window, "to let the soul fly away". Objectively, it was not a heartbreaking night, but it's as if a seed had been sown that would later turn into pain. The plant began growing at the funeral. As shame. I could feel people's pity. "Poor kid, he's lost his father." Then came the rage at my brother for crying. He was showing his grief, not me. Later, there was the fear of not being protected, the sadness at my mother's loneliness, the emptiness... The thousand faces of suffering. And that's when I felt that tearing, that wrenching in my guts. I was twelve. It was June 18, 1948. His death was not the climax of my pain, it was a time bomb.

Take Care of Yourself

I received an email telling me it was over. I didn't know how to respond.
It was almost as if it hadn't been meant for me. It ended with the words,
"Take care of yourself." And so I did. I asked 107 women (including two
made from wood and one with feathers), chosen for their profession or
skills, to interpret this letter. To analyze it, comment on it, dance it, sing it.
Dissect it. Exhaust it. Understand it for me.
Answer for me.
It was a way of taking the time to break up.
A way of taking care of myself.

Tango singer, Débora Russ

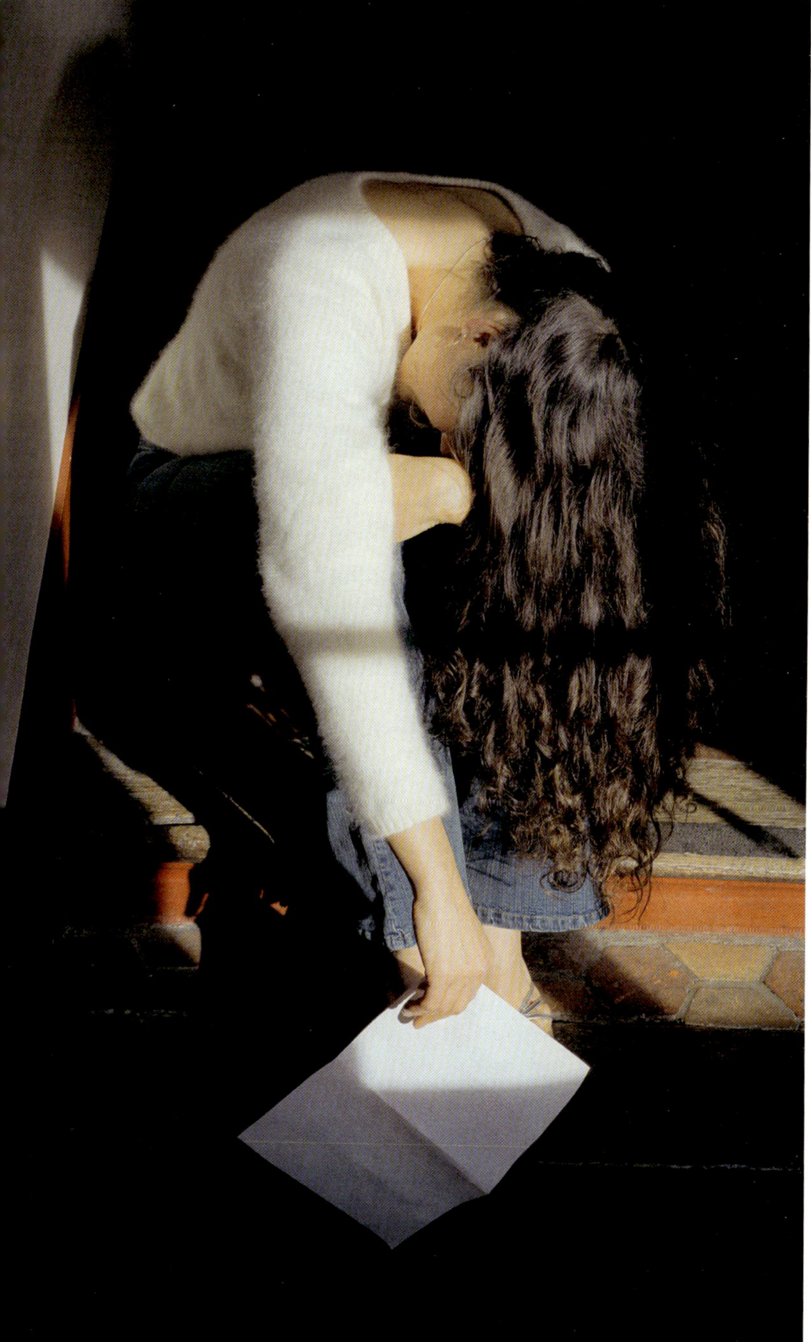

Punctuation: I have changed
it only where necessary.

Change all apostrophes ' ' → ' '
Change all quote marks " " → " "

Long ill-constructed
sentence

Clumsy sentence
opening

Short repetitious text. I have
joined up all the repetitions
and highlighted in orange all
the conjugations of the verb
"to know" and in yellow, all the
conjugations of the verb "to tell"

Awkward repetition

Flush right

Proofreader, Valérie Lermite

Sophie,

Cela fait un moment que je veux vous écrire et répondre à votre dernier mail. En même temps, il me semblait préférable de vous parler et de dire ce que j'ai à vous dire de vive voix.

Mais du moins cela sera-t-il écrit.

Comme vous l'avez vu, j'allais mal tous ces derniers temps. Comme si je ne me retrouvais plus dans ma propre existence. Une sorte d'angoisse terrible contre laquelle je ne peux pas grand-chose, sinon aller de l'avant pour tenter de la prendre de vitesse, comme j'ai toujours fait.

Lorsque nous nous sommes rencontrés, vous aviez posé une condition : ne pas devenir la "quatrième". J'ai tenu cet engagement : cela fait des mois que j'ai cessé de voir les "autres", ne trouvant évidemment aucun moyen de les voir sans faire de vous l'une d'elles.

Je croyais que cela suffirait, je croyais que vous aimer et que votre amour suffiraient pour que l'angoisse qui me pousse toujours à aller voir ailleurs et m'empêche à jamais d'être tranquille et sans doute simplement heureux et "généreux" se calmerait à votre contact et dans la certitude que l'amour que vous me portez était le plus bénéfique pour moi, le plus bénéfique que j'ai jamais connu, vous le savez. J'ai cru que l'écriture serait un remède, mon "intranquillité" s'y dissolvant pour vous retrouver. Mais non. C'est même devenu encore pire : je ne peux même pas vous dire dans quel état je me sens en moi-même. Alors, cette semaine, j'ai commencé à rappeler les "autres". Et je sais ce que cela veut dire pour moi et dans quel cycle cela va m'entraîner.

Je ne vous ai jamais menti et ce n'est pas aujourd'hui que je vais commencer.

Il y avait une autre règle que vous aviez posée au début de notre histoire : le jour où nous cesserions d'être amants, me voir ne serait plus envisageable pour vous. Vous savez comme cette contrainte ne peut que me paraître désastreuse, injuste (alors que vous voyez toujours B., R.,...) et compréhensible (évidemment...) ; ainsi je ne pourrais jamais devenir votre ami.

Mais aujourd'hui, vous pouvez mesurer l'importance de ma décision au fait que je sois prêt à me plier à votre volonté, alors que ne plus vous voir ni vous parler ni saisir votre regard sur les choses et les êtres et votre douceur sur moi me manqueront infiniment.

Quoi qu'il arrive, sachez que je ne cesserai de vous aimer de cette manière qui fut la mienne dès que je vous ai connue et qui se prolongera en moi et, je le sais, ne mourra pas.

Mais aujourd'hui, ce serait la pire des mascarades que de maintenir une situation que vous savez aussi bien que moi devenue irrémédiable au regard même de cet amour que je vous porte et de celui que vous me portez et qui m'oblige encore à cette franchise envers vous, comme dernier gage de ce qui fut entre nous et restera unique.

J'aurais aimé que les choses tournent autrement.

Prenez soin de vous.

Letter coded using the Vigenère encryption system. The keyword chosen for the encryption was "Rupture."

C KLFOVAN ZX NIJEX SI SYIMYI XF NPEE KS PIJ THU XVFA RIL AYUI B BRZV
ND LUP SLN AHOU WKCAE UK PVUHM CK AZFA UY NVZNIXHRW PIJ AUMI
EIIBWVH Z BPOY ESK VTXH MIIS LXFC ME GNLYCJ IYRXHKPP UH BZ Z RF
FDGAVV IYRHAEMJYS FSJICZ XG GP SNH TQCJXVHRX U KIILXUFV JVYABHX SW
UCQCVXP QWBWY M TUCGIK VVUAES WMXBI HNYII NWTH BIVJXGA FR XIXGA
KS KLN THU SMYGMUBI ZN PL C RPNUNL BRZV XDGY NLVH LX GVX PIJ EUZH
UILG IEI TICWCKMFH CHN KS SYRHGV XYY UHOIXY C HMIFH SS IAUK TIIBBMV
MK BPL VVIE GDGNYW EIL LCEGV C WTPV WVYC MBV SKBTKM SITUJLY Z
SSPXHOJPP WDNFU JZHS GI NEP IU LYVMEA IAYD AZNWHOK QREXGA PSL
ICX IW XYYBB NYSLAWM NYEK QDNFU FV YCHOXL Z NWHOXLK NWTN PSL
FDOYU EEX IAUK CFOG EIMI NIJEX SI VHDNAY WF NWTN KLZM PGRZIKS
LACTL TICLNRRKFN WLZZVM BX NF PFIZ YOIXYYG TZZICX PGX NLZWW FYRRJ
C LBFC RVPTK VV EK LTLN FV GLDUUSPP YKXH AYJN WTJGC FL VXHVVFOH
PILPU VT VUCQVX LAYE M NUH PCKL PIJ PCKL KBT VYIXRCCMS KLRN IAY
CSMY NHO YEMY UHL DI NUH MBV FVMI YII QV NWX VVWK C WTPV IMYG AUU
CFO ZGIN XYUI B NYSLAWM NYEK QGBNZRX QDNFU FV U GXGVHP NWTN DC
IYHMFVWJHTLM NSLFS WCJWFFKX CEXF CI LI KLRN X VILPU ZXGX PSL VJM
HF ME ZPVN ZX VPTG VVGRGT PIIWV C RTHESK YKXH KICF NHO KLV MDKN FJ
JNPMY Z JVYA B UD ME MD B MKEINTW WRPCCCZ NYI FNWXLJ EXUXG NYMJ
QTXE RRU C ZGIN AYUI MBRX DYPGM KS DY PGX KLV WNVFV XYUI BN NMCF
SKUX QV CCMIZ LRPT GYMII FXXX KS PIJ THU M UI CHN ZRKYCW NF WKUGM
FPMEA CHQKLVLT PUJ EEIIAYI VLFT MBRX PIJ EUZH UILG UK XYY QXAZRECCZ
IW SLL PYZRMI NWX XRC NY HMIGTVX QXCEK CIKXLJ CFO LHOCH EI AHHXII
VT TVCI KI TGPZWRAT LYVMEA BX SFY BHDP NYMJ WDGMKVRCCM WRR
FHAR YMII MIKCBI DY PL XZWRMIKILW RHS NHAYJN LAYE CFO HMCCP JYT
U UEH I UCW OEHVLHMUEHRVAX ISZZIJLFP WF C RTH EIMYG UYTSDY NHOI
JICTGXSYK HDP SFY TUC ZULKV BDP MZKECUBWRRK GN WYTMJCDG CJ JIIB
MBV JRWI MBRX Z UB ILVTRLTW NF FVHS MI PSLL LBFC IMYC MBFYXB IAYII RLT
LI DEES IACEKJ HDM MVIZHV RIL SI NPEEZRX ND RIL SI WPMWYMEA IAY NEP
SDN FFSB UI IYFTCY PGX KLZHVL UEH PIJK AVRKFTGYJW KILTLUW DY IAUK M
NCAE GZWJ NTKLZFCSLAUKIMYG AUGTVHH KYDIDVTK NYEK C LBFC ECQPRM
CSMY NHO ZR KBT LUDI NUN FS FAE QPR C YEMY TOYI WZHRX C WMIMI FYK
CFO IAUK MK QXEF TEILN HH NMKBXG GV EEX X TG JYIY LBFC RVPTK XZI SOI
BN NSLFS UY KLV QDKMK OZHS HZ DEJKJXLRHV ND ILFPFHV T MZXLUIBIE
RFQ LAYE CFO ZGIN EJ QTEF RW Z XD BN YEJ VTVIDI ZLGXJRVRVAX VP XYY
HMUEHRLSL IW XYY KXLP PFPT B BRZV ZDK SFY RHS RIL LRPT YII QV U AHPV
AYCRA CJ RFQ UHLTMEA BX NF FV MD YLRRB QXMB PSL UH YCEEC JGHIW SW
QWTN YEGJTGYU FVNLXYE YJ UCW QZPC UAPUPW SY JGCHYVC LHOCH YUKX
FZOVX IACEKJ ND AUMI KOGGYU SLN SBZWIIYCMFPXRET VUII FZ NHOIWVFU
Q

DGSE intelligence officer, Louise

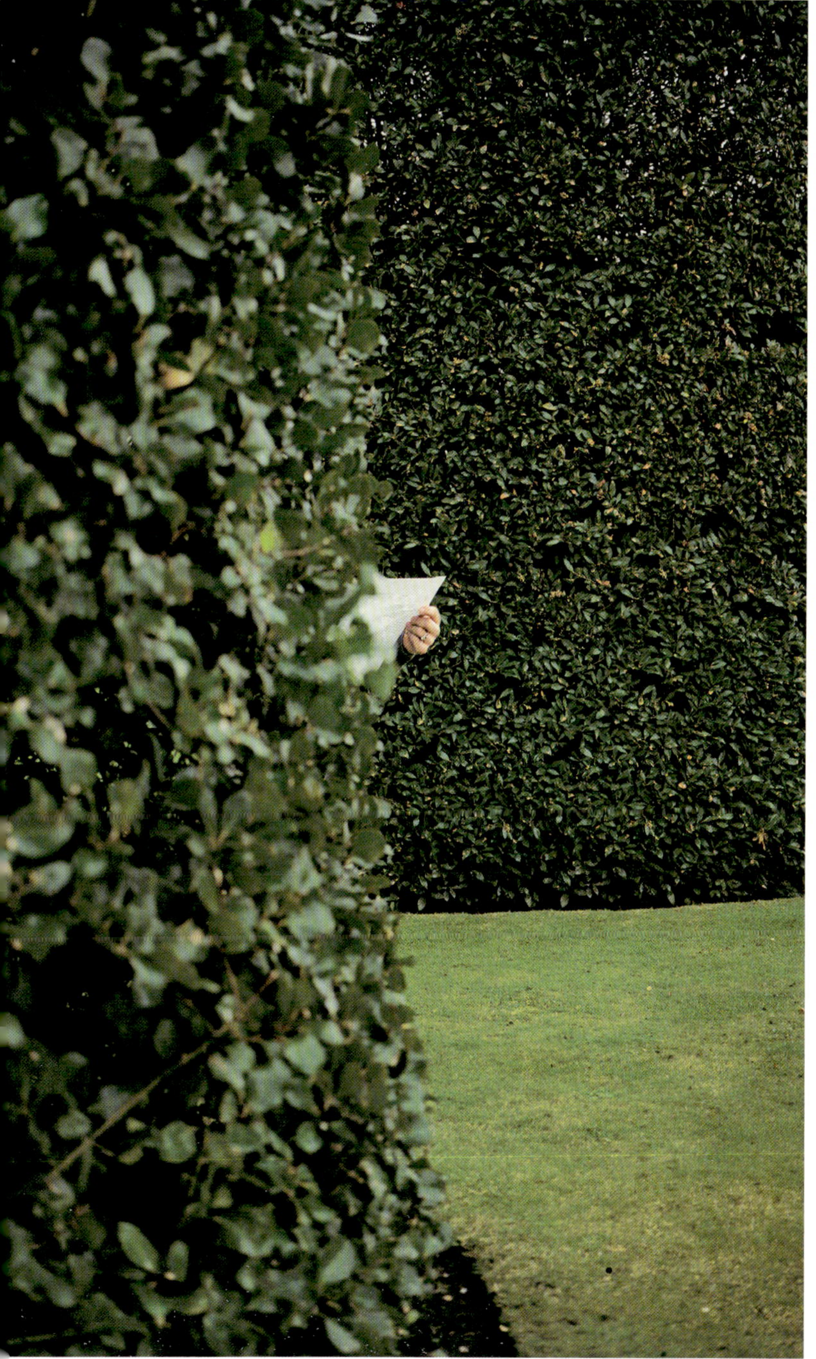

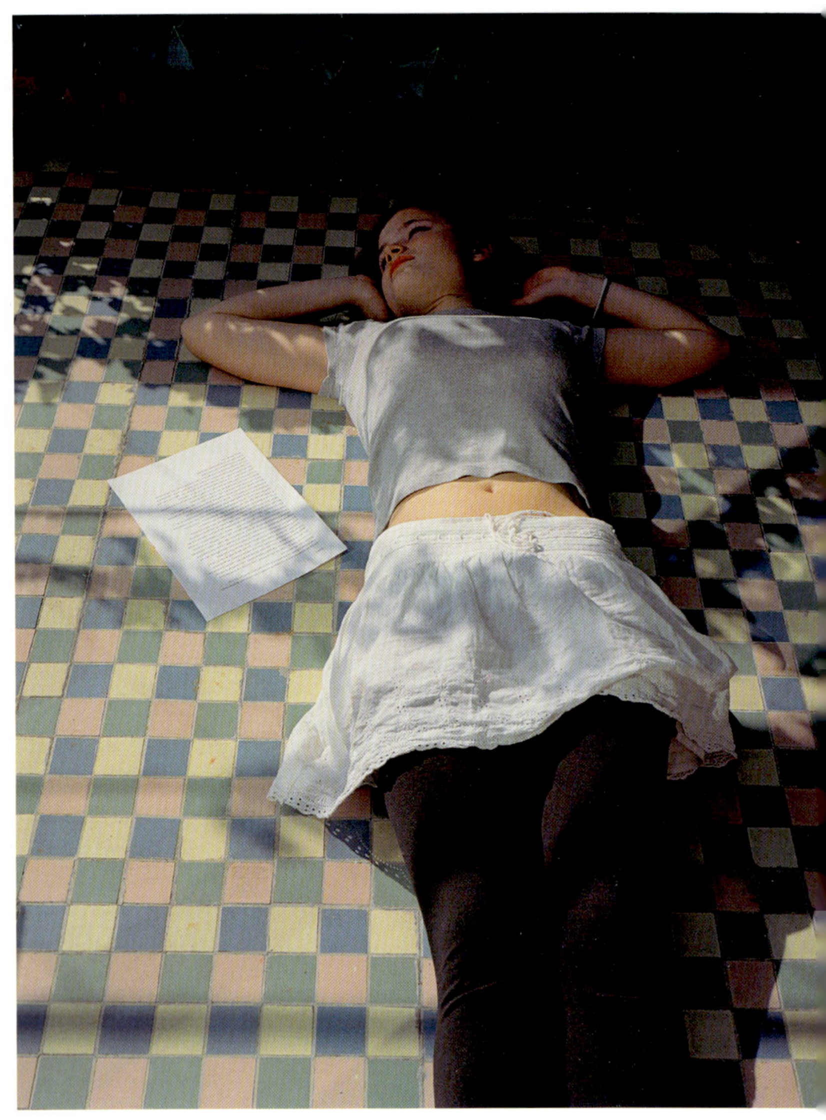

Teenager, Anna Bouguereau

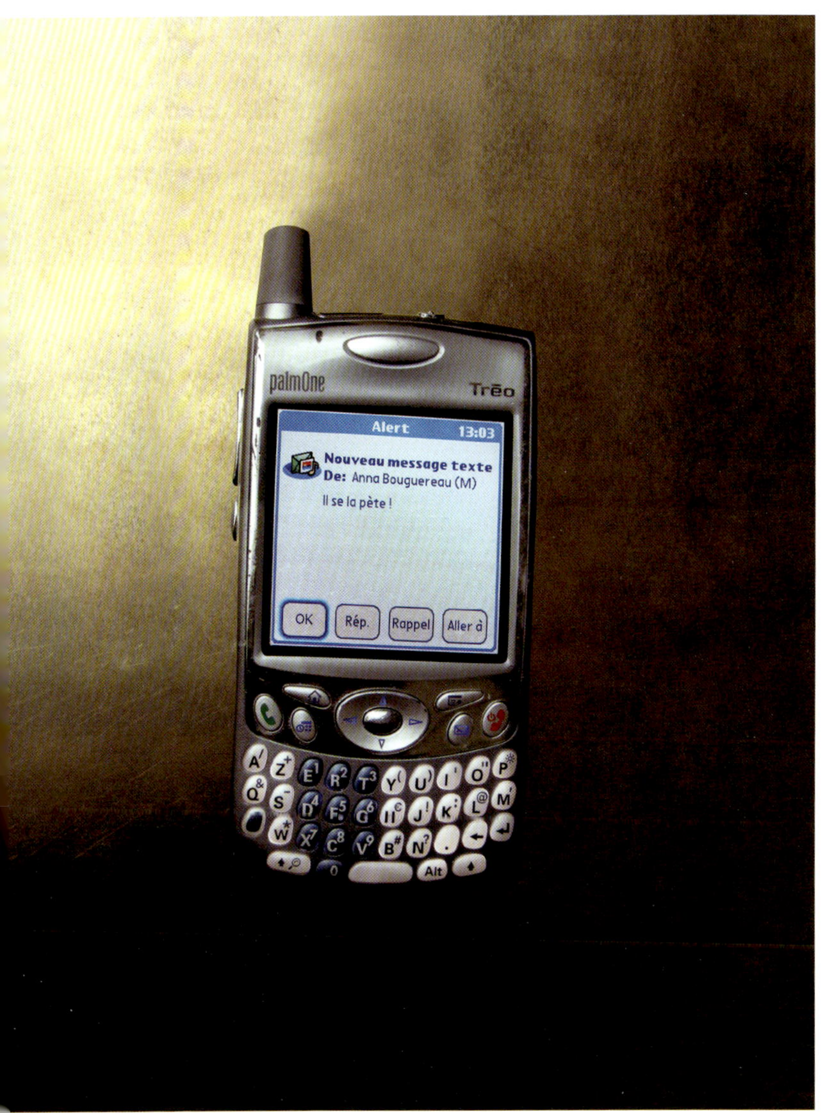

Text message from Anna Bouguereau:
"He thinks he's cool!"

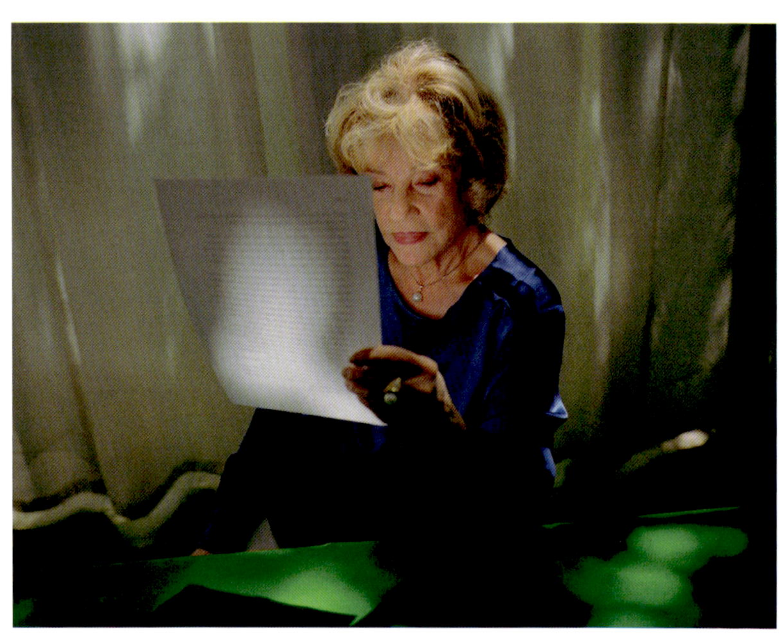

Actress, Jeanne Moreau

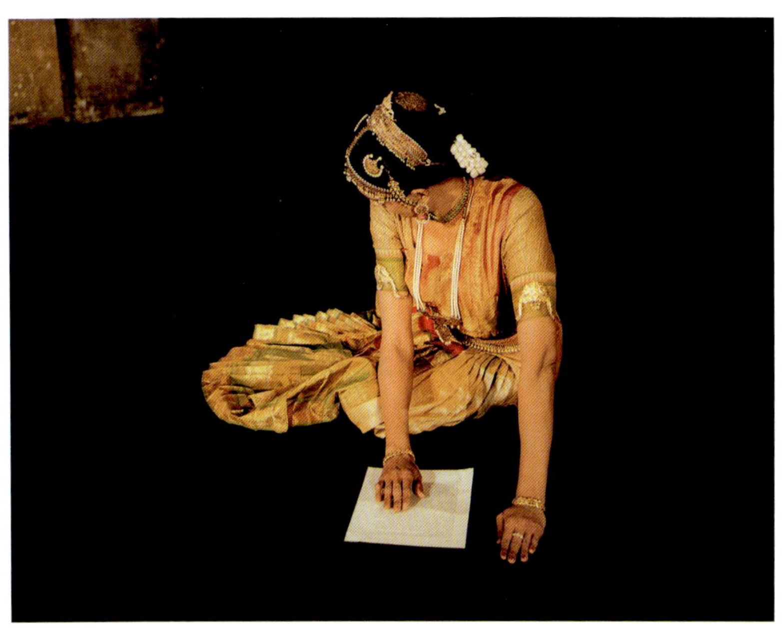

Bharatanatyam dancer, Priyadarsini Govind

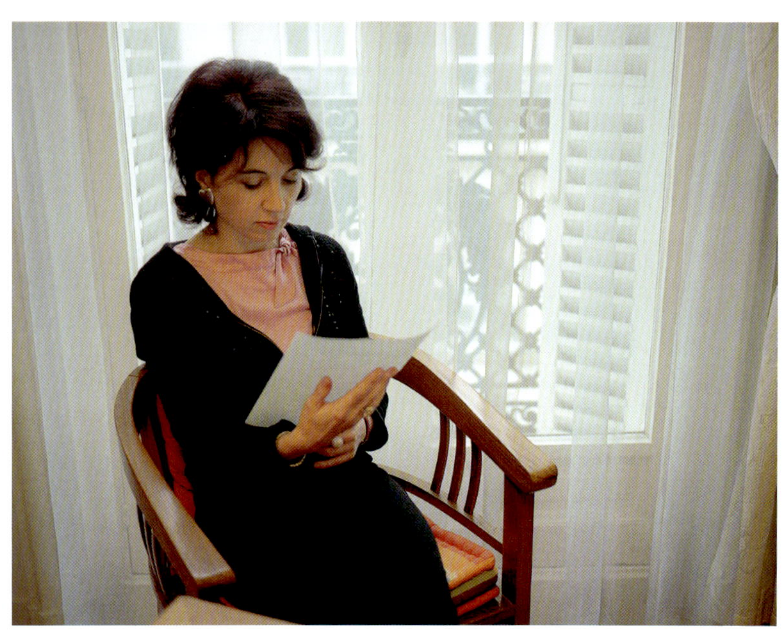

Sexologist, Catherine Solano

**Groupe Hospitalier
Cochin-Saint-Vincent-de-Paul
La Roche-Guyon**

27, rue du Faubourg Saint-Jacques
75679 PARIS Cedex 14

Téléphone : 01.58.41.27.53
Fax : 01.58.41.27.85

N° F.I.N.E.S.S. : 750100166

**SERVICE D'UROLOGIE
(Bâtiment ALBARRAN)**
Tél. : 01.58.41.27.53

Chef de Service
Pr Bernard DEBRÉ

Dr : Cathere SOCANO
Fonction : attachée
Tél. :
N° Adeli :

3M03014

Date : 1er juin 2004

Nom et Prénom du patient :
Sophie CALLE
Age : 1953

Non, je ne vois pas de
raison de vous prescrire
des anti dépresseurs. Vous êtes
simplement triste.
Un évènement douloureux, ça
fait mal, mais la solution nor-
male n'est pas chimique.
Vous avez certainement assez de force
pour aller de l'avant et trouver en
vous des ressources pour agir et
réagir -

Signature :

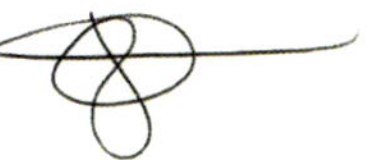

No, I don't see any reason to prescribe antidepressants for you. You are simply sad. A distressing event is bound to hurt, but the appropriate solution is not a chemical one. I'm sure you are strong enough to move on and find within yourself the resources to act and react.

On the Hunt

Rules of the game. A catalogue of the main qualities sought by men in female partners, and by women in male partners, as seen through a selection of lonely hearts advertisements published in *Le Chasseur français* between 1895 and 2010.

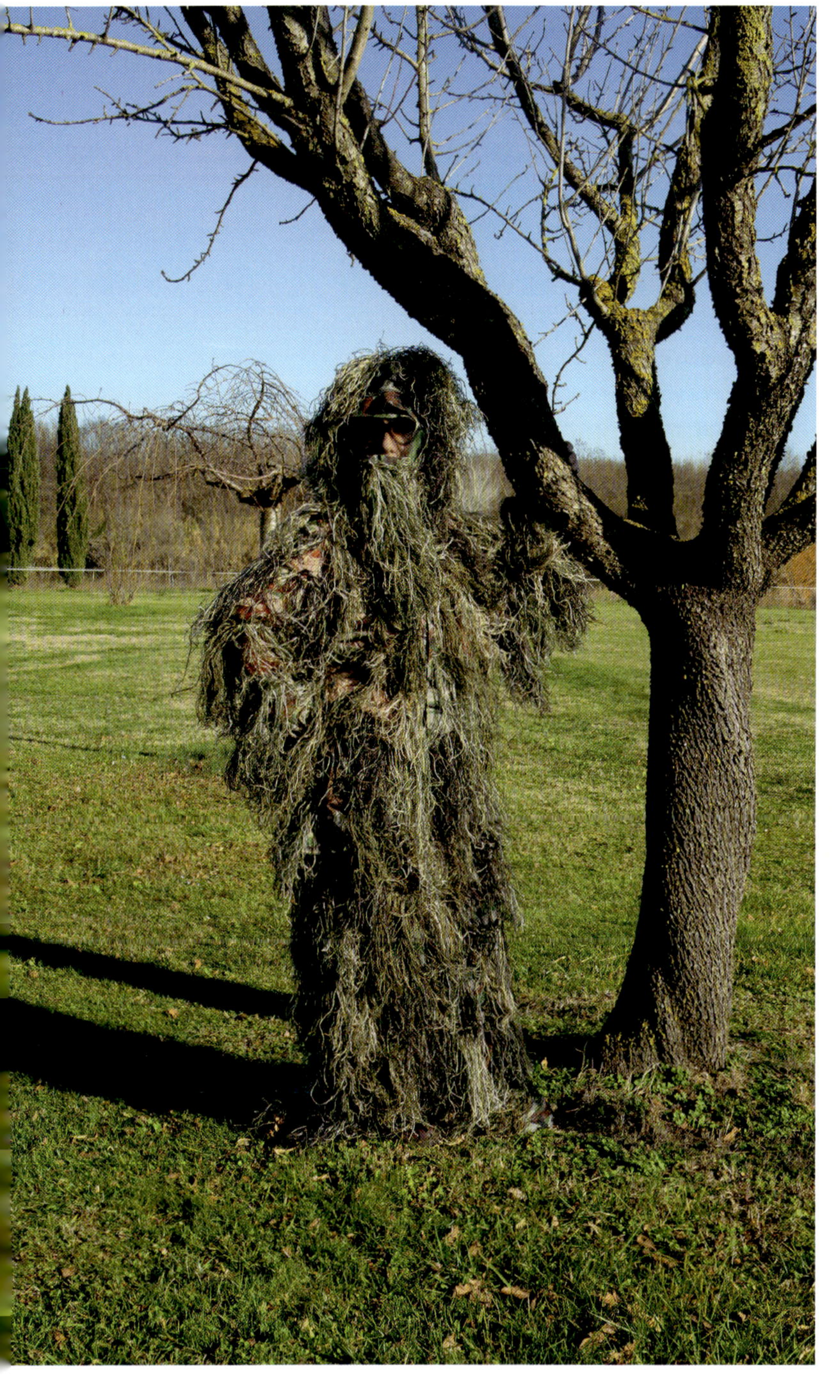

1905–1914

With or without stain

Gentleman of leisure seeks lady of means. Would ignore any stain if good dowry. | Young man 25 years old no relatives and Catholic would like to meet a deaf-mute woman from a good family. | Indigent boy, 23 years old, wishes to marry an indigent girl, even with stain. | Single man 43 years old, good, slightly rheumatic, wishes to marry a lady of leisure or landowner in an area abounding in game, even if ill, would share the suffering. | Seeking a very well brought-up young girl, good and simple, very honest and very upstanding, dowry essential unfortunately a necessity of life. | Single man, 28 years old, honorable family, vineyard owner, income 4,000, would marry now or in a few years young lady, deformed, crippled, not a socialite, wealthy, having encountered many setbacks. | Young man 34 years old, handsome chap, income 7,000 francs, good situation, would marry young lady with equivalent fortune. Would tolerate stain. | Officer 30 years old nobleman with title would marry very honorable, very rich young lady, without stain. | Young Belgian man, 36 years old, 20,000 francs, would marry young girl between 18 to 30 years old, with or without stain, either pretty or wealthy. | Gentleman 36 years old, with advanced diploma, bored of being alone, wishes to correspond with a view to marry nice little madame without stain and with some wealth. | Gentleman 32 years old, would like to get to know very simple girl for marriage. | Single man 35 years old, impeccable past, from an old and honorable family, would marry robust young lady. Delicate health please abstain. | Landowner, 24 years old, secure situation in horticulture-husbandry, seeking young girl with simple tastes, some wealth and good health. | Widowed shopkeeper, 31 years old, would marry widow even infirm owning 9,000 francs. | Affectionate young man, good situation, would marry young lady in good health, who likes greengrocer business. | Gentleman, 49 years old, with title, Earl, very good, 8,000 income, seeking woman with equivalent situation. | Landowner 48 years old, good, with references, income 1,300 francs, would marry well-to-do lady. Would pass over stain, family, infirmity. | Young man, 24 years old, nobleman, Catholic, intelligent and hardworking, seeking young lady without stain, 19 to 24 years old, raised on a farm. | Single man 56 years old has suffered a lot would marry lady with big heart. Any region.

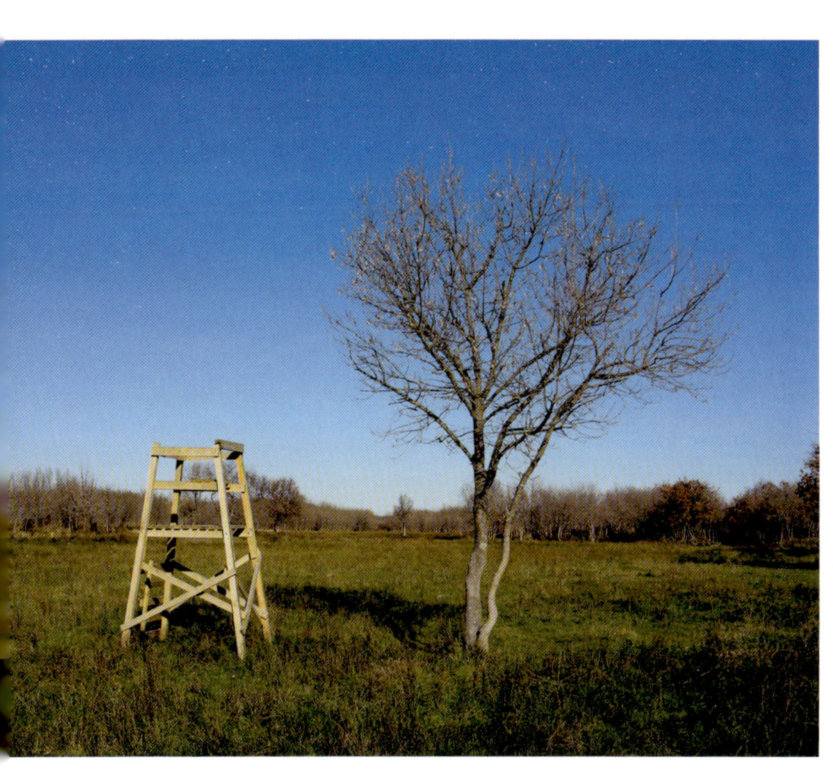

1905–1914

Wealthy even if ugly

Sincerely serious advertisement: lady 45 years old having encountered great setbacks, fond of elderly men. Will she find one? Octogenarian, infirm, ugly, whatever. As a reward for the fortune that he will bring, this lady will be the ideal companion for old age and will show him great affection. | 47 years old, distinguished, wishes to become the married companion of a very elderly and very rich gentleman, without children even illegitimate, bored of being alone with his more or less dedicated servants. He will be assured of the best care. | Beautiful young girl 23 years old, very organised housekeeper, wishing to develop product without competition, would marry a worker with 15,000 francs. | Little typist 24 years old, nice physique, would correspond with a tall gentleman from the construction industry or dentist. | Lady from Amiens in the Somme, 34 years old, orphan, 9 million, would marry anyone with good situation who would ignore stain. | Poor young lady would marry wealthy man, elderly or infirm. | Widow 38 years old, true owner of 200,000, would marry very elderly gentleman even if ugly with very very big fortune. Send stamp. | Young woman of the world, having been disappointed, seeks tender girlfriend, well-to-do, any age. | respectable family seeks Catholic veterinary doctor for nice young girl 21 years old. Would pass over smaller income. Possibility to take over customers. | Parents wish to marry girl 27 years old, acceptable physique, very docile, remarkable pianist, with well brought-up gentleman 32-45 years old with portfolio fortune. | 26 and 23 years old, good housekeepers, with good talents that earn a living, would marry workers without defects. | Lady 30 years old, no dowry but hardworking, would marry someone of modest means. Wouldn't mind living countryside. | Brunette with blue eyes, 23 years old, keen to marry nice young man, 25-32 years old, good-looking, profession with a return of 3,000 per year with prospect of pay rise. | Lady with a noble heart, 45 years old, descendant of Napoléon 1st seeks pious gentleman, very old, very rich, with a title of nobility. I say very old because would in marriage only want a good companion. | Lady 37 years old living in a melancholic hamlet, wishes to correspond with a rich gentleman in his autumn years. | To ladies wishing to marry will offer addresses of wealthy gentlemen.

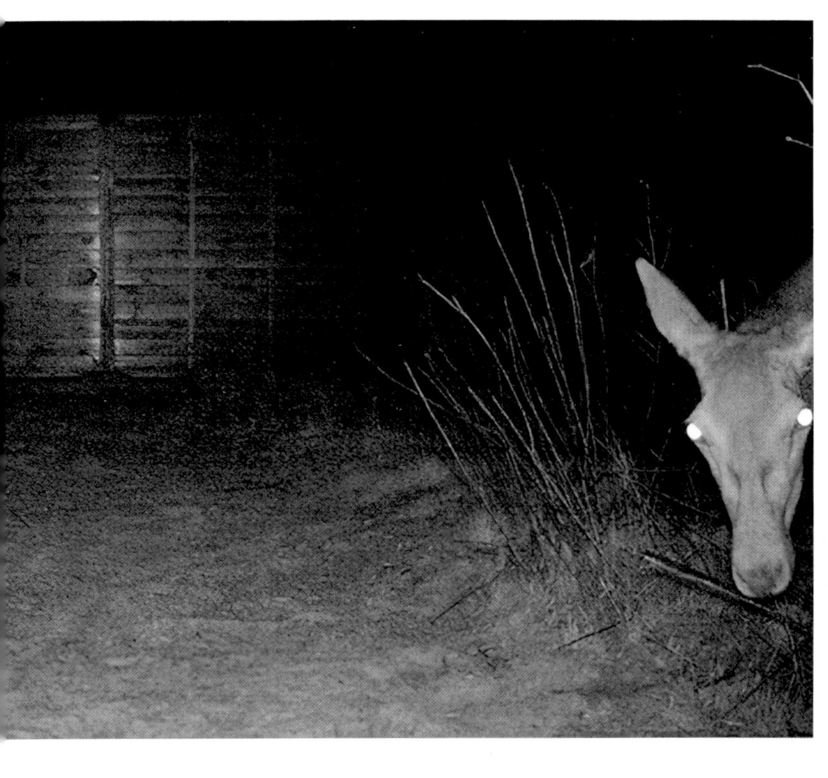

1950–1960

A good catch, able to replace dead mother

South of France. Retired man 300,000 young-looking, normal physique, 1st prize in Fine Arts, owner of 8 houses, alone with 80 year old father, seeks 40 year old soulmate, with great quality of the heart, able to replace dead mother. | Non-practising Southerner 55, in good health, building valued at 4 million, would like to meet a person in the dairy business. | Talented DPLG architect, lacking connections, would marry daughter of an architect or entrepreneur. | Divorced, 47 years old, shopkeeper, owner, car, sober, Catholic, without children, would correspond with women of a similar age, minimum 1,200,000 to pay ex-wife allowance. | Former industrialist, setback, 70 years old, 76 kg 1 m 74, sober frugal healthy car, would correspond with gentle understanding landlady owning a house with small outbuildings for a peaceful end of life. | Gentleman 48 years old normal divorced hotelier 5 million car wishes to correspond with disinterested and serious lady capable of managing a hotel.| Distinguished single man, divorced, Catholic, French, excellent family, having experienced setback, would correspond with a view to marriage, distinguished young woman who is a homeowner or will bring funds to buy a property. Solicitor or priest accepted as intermediary. | Complicated young man 27 years old average health poor seeks ideal young girl. | Single, 45, metalworker, wishes to correspond with a housekeeping and farming lady. | Single, 30, good physique, health, serious, loyal, perfect morals, BE certificate, would marry young woman maximum 30 years old, pleasant physique, health, irreproachable morals, with possibility to help him obtain a situation in colonies. Adventuress please abstain. | Model maker, production manager, single, 33 years old, friendly, 1 m 80, slim, practising Catholic, able to head technical department of a womenswear or menswear clothing factory, would like to meet young girl, tall, elegant, affectionate, parents in the clothing industry for collaboration. | Practising Catholic farmer seeks wife, 20-30, with capital to buy building in Lourdes. | Single man, serious, good in all respects, 1 m 84, experienced manager, high references, holdings 7,500,000, would marry serious, tall, slim, pretty, 37-43 years old bringing industry or business with good income.

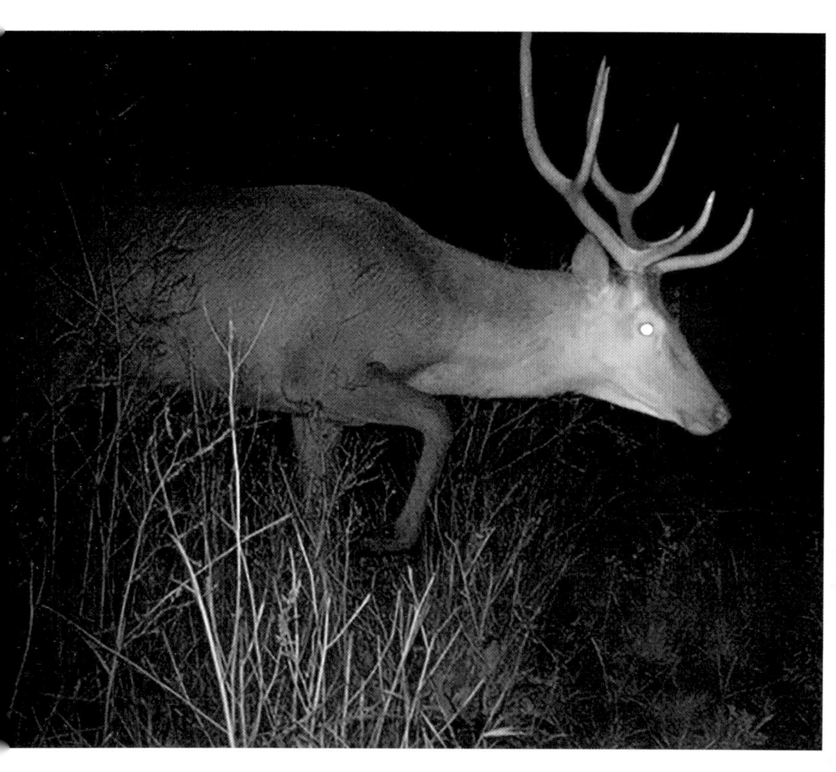

1950–1960

Essentially kind and gentle

33 years old, war widow, upper middle class, 5 children, seeks exceptional widower not stingy wintering in Nice to replace late father. Minimum 1 million. | Widow of cattle trader, possibly good collaborator, cannot offer anything else, would marry kind physically diminished 40, excessively gentle, not difficult, not demanding. | Is a young woman 42 allowed to dream future happiness with a SNCF agent 44-50? | Tired solitude, nurseryman widow would escape to marry poetic soul 55-58 good presentation and end her days among animals and flowers. I have enough to buy house and garden that could have space for the former and the latter. | True young lady 23 years old would marry baker or butcher. Short men please abstain. | Who, from a respectable background, good, disinterested, would marry kind person a little childish despite 34 years old, sickly, without fortune, without house, without relatives? Preferably former scout. | Alert. Divorced from philandering doctor, 550,000 pension + liquid assets, house furnished adequately, seeks great personality without conceit, 32-45, clean, healthy, free but gentle. Obese, bald, don't bother. | 54 years old, without useful connections, 4 CV car, plush apartment in Le Havre, seeks chic young man, normal physique, non smoker non drinker, very clean. Preferably bricklayer. | Chatelaine 68 marvelously young, anti-concordat, ash blond greying hair uncut naturally curly, superb chompers, pleasant faults, strong qualities, seeks remarkable soul for sweet autumn. | Grocery shopkeeper, 43, pleasant ensemble, good revenue, slight swaying walk, comfortable car, married daughter, would make gentle and serious gentleman happy. Shared costs and profits. | Seeking M 50 good appearance absolutely not lazy, practical knowledge of heating engineering, plumbing, central heating. | Single mum not bad, neglected by unscrupulous Y M, 24, maid, seeking Catholic radio-electrician. | Polytechnician daughter having had setbacks, expecting baby in November, seeks sweet happiness with good gentleman. Would accept non-contagious disability morally compensated. Indecisive please abstain. | For my daughter, 26, more pleasant than pretty, slightly irregular face, 15 million dowry, father garage Paris, seeks mechanic son-in-law spotless past.

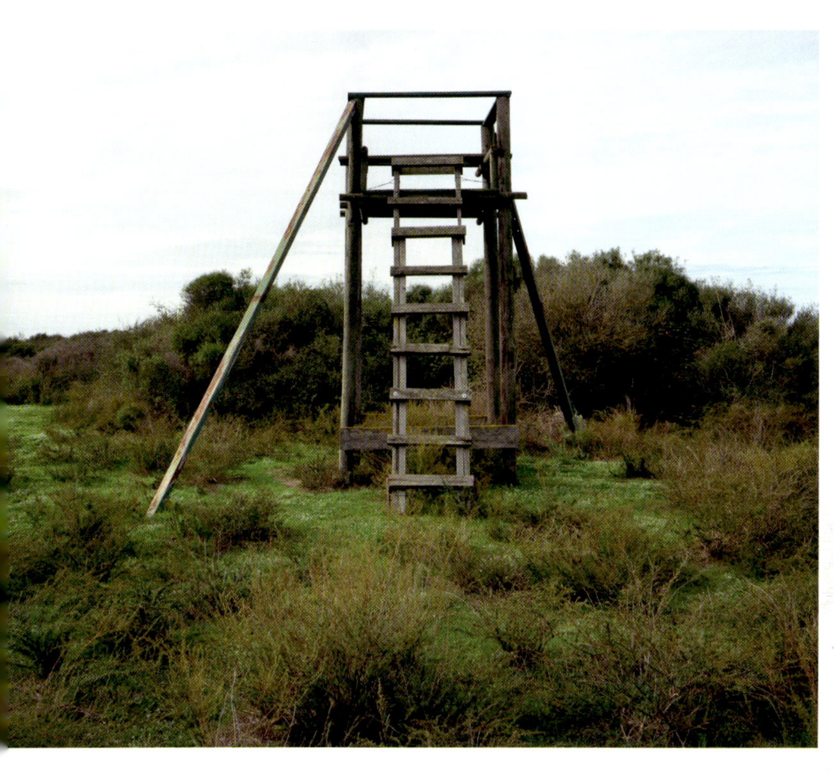

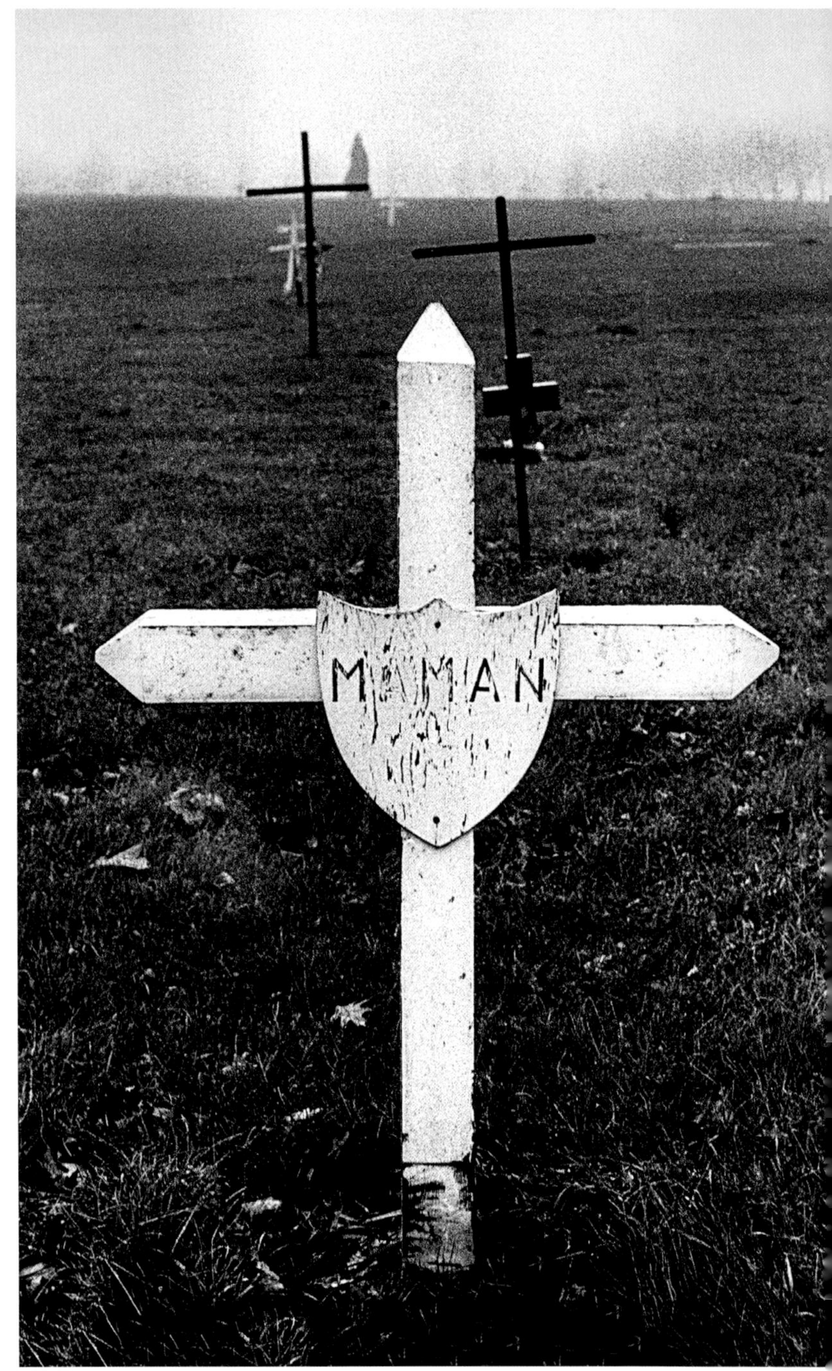

MAMAN

Sad Stories

Autobiographies, 1998–2020…

Dead in a Good Mood

Read in my mother's diary:

December 28, 1985. No use investing in the tenderness of my children, between Antoine's placid indifference and Sophie's selfish arrogance! My only consolation is, she is so morbid that she will come visit me in my grave more often than on Rue Boulard.

May 29, 1986. I don't remember to whom I said yesterday over the phone, about myself: "She came from nothing—and left jaded about everything!"

September 9, 1986. I still don't know whether I want to be cremated or buried. Funny how I can't imagine that happening to me at all!

April 28, 1987. Good-bye, Diary! I'm off to New York. Let's hope it will all be wonderful. If the plane crashes, here's a cheery farewell to life!

November 10, 1988. I slowly get used to my depression; slighted, it slowly backs away.

June 6, 1989. Abominable.

January 1, 1990. "To have accomplished nothing and to die overworked." (Cioran)

April 1, 1990. No, I'm not depressed, nor bitter, but I am terribly bored, without purpose or project or vision, "I feel that I am just a ruined tomb in which my virtues and illusions lie."

February 21, 1995. Nothing! Except nursing my sorrow.

December 11, 1995. I would already like Christmas to be over. Or perhaps I'd like my life to be over.

December 10, 1996. Dear Diary (possibly the last volume thereof), good-bye. I didn't give you much, and you returned the compliment …

One of the notebooks was undated and the pages were blank, except for a few notes about how to use the VCR, and this sentence: "I died in a very good mood."

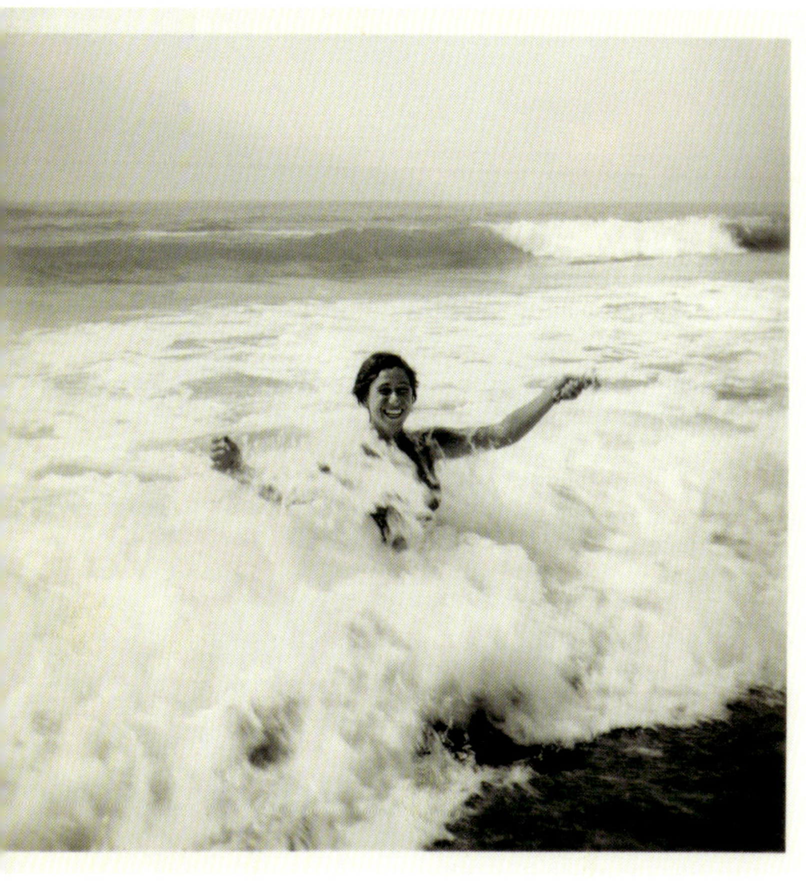

Today My Mother Died

On December 27, 1986, my mother wrote in her diary: "My mother died today."

On March 15, 2006, in turn, I wrote in mine: "My mother died today."

No one will say this about me.

The end.

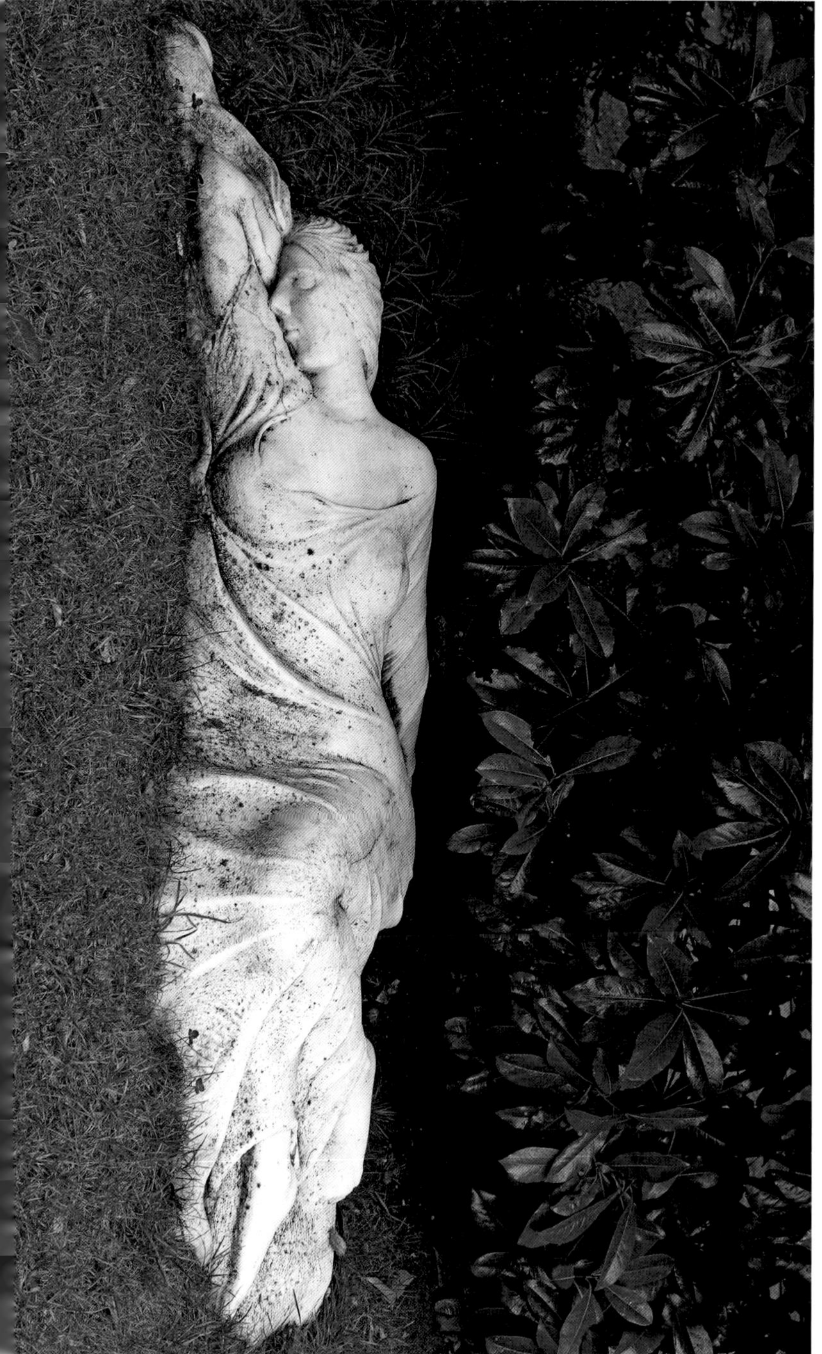

The ghost of Souris

Dear Sophie, I recently heard about the deaths of your cat and your father, and I just wanted to let you know I was thinking about you. M. Souris is the name that I will have repeated most often in my life. I still catch myself whispering it at night. His preferred territory was the space between my two pillows. There, in that void, that stillness where he used to breathe, I feel his absence most keenly. After our fathers die, we don't sleep with their ghosts in our beds.

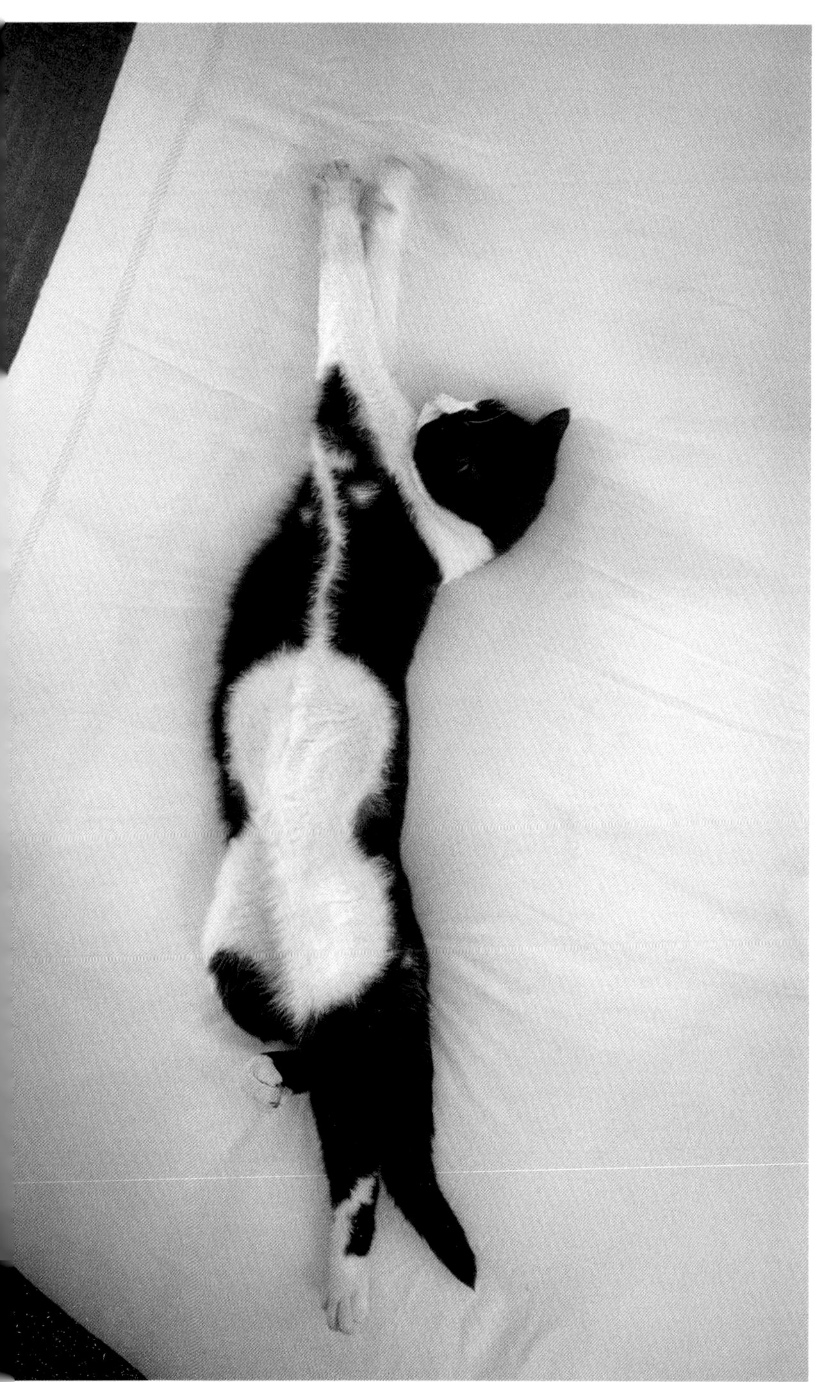

Souris

Fabio kissed him. Camille whispered her song, "She Was", into his ear. Florence stroked him. Anne put him to sleep. He died. Maurice dug a hole in the garden. I laid Souris in a little white model coffin, the kind travelling sales reps would use before the advent of photography. Too small. His back paws were sticking out. Yves buried him. Serena planted daffodils around his grave.

I received a message on my phone: *Sophie, I am sorry about your cat. Could you ask Camille to pick up some vegetables maybe leeks or turnips if she sees any? Kisses.*

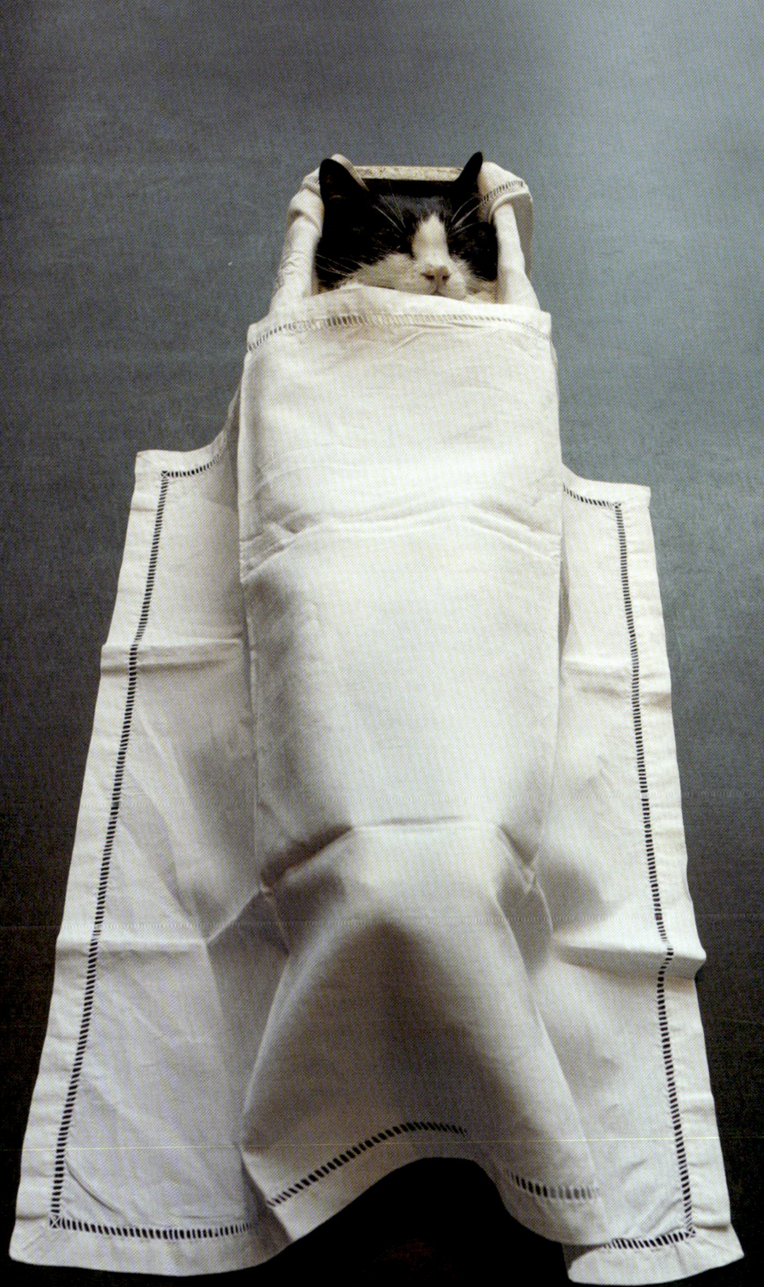

Silent Heart Attack

When my father fell ill, I too fell ill. I got shingles and had a heart attack.
As if I wanted my father, a doctor, to take care of his daughter one last
time. Or as though I were accompanying him on his way, wedding myself
to his illness, while at the same time, through this irreproachable excuse,
avoiding the sight of him in his diminished state.

To reiterate.

Shingles: weakened immune system. Heart attack: death of a part of the
heart. Unlike the usual heart attack, mine was "*silent*". Was the imminent
loss of those eyes that had guided my life threatening me with silence?

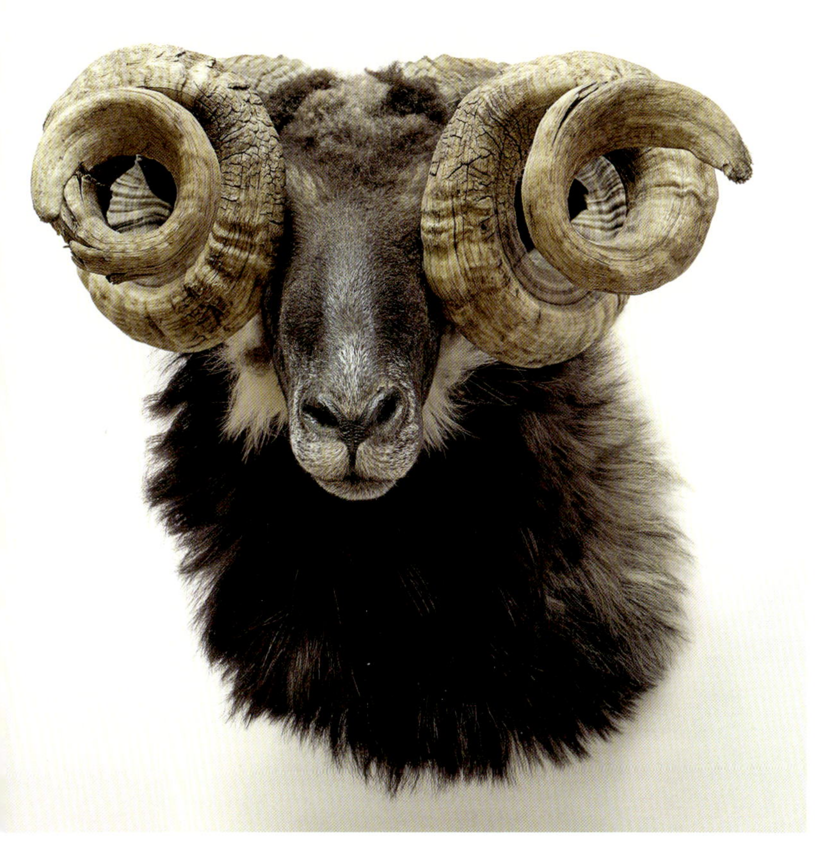

Morning

Each night, after leaving his hospital room, I would write down what might be my father's last word.

There was: elsewhere, homosexual, money.

Whispered: I can't go on.

Who's there? Glass of wine. Cypress.

That week, on Monday, he said: Screwed.

Tuesday: Daughter. "This is my daughter." Something I'll never hear again.

Wednesday, with a movement of his lips and eyes, he asked for a kiss. My father, who never kissed me, wanted a kiss. Could this very uncharacteristic gesture be his last word?

Thursday: Toilets. Not a great word. He would be alive tomorrow, for sure.

Friday: Paintings. "We're going to rehang the paintings."

A beautiful last word. A dangerous one. I was torn between wanting a perfect final word, and hoping for a bad word, a word that could not be the last, one that would reassure me that my father would be alive tomorrow.

Saturday, he said: Dying.

Sunday, he said: Morning.

He died on Monday April 6, 2015, at 6.50 am.

My father was ninety-four years old.

Not long before, when I asked him how he was doing, he responded: "I'm not making any progress."

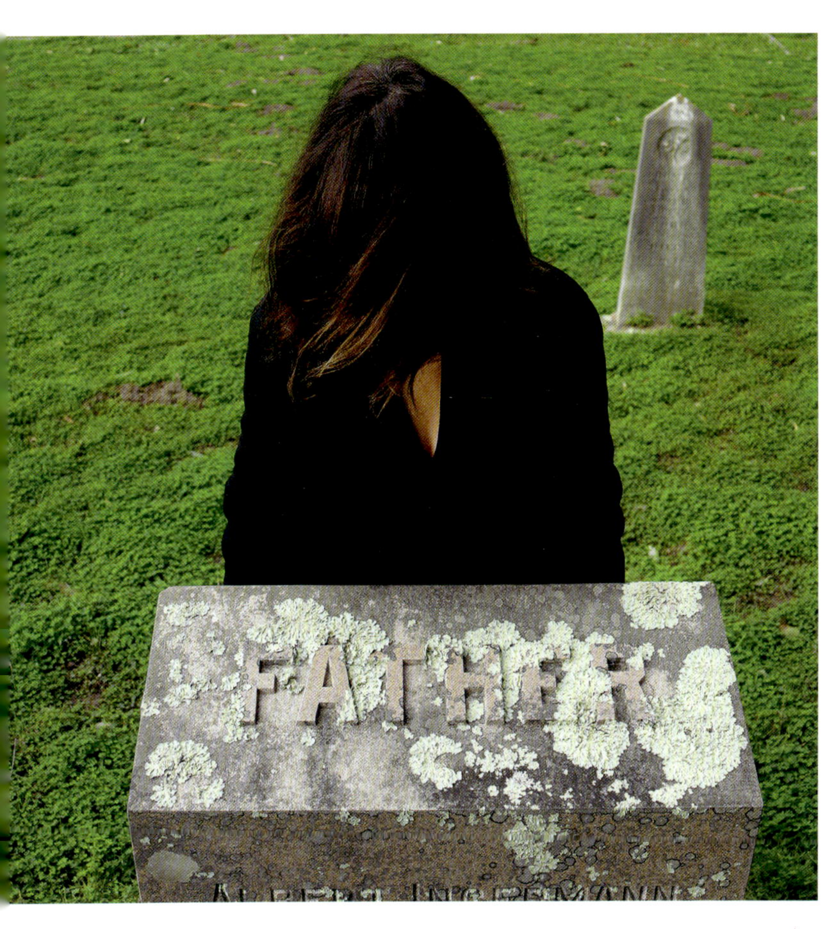
FATHER

My Mother, My Cat, My Father

My parents each took three months to die. Three months: time for the last gestures of love, time to become an orphan. But not the endless, grinding time of agony and despair, of seeing my flamboyant mother and my impeccable father fall from their heights.

A week before she died, my mother refused to see an unwelcome visitor: "Tell him I'm dead!" On the Tuesday before he died, my father complained: "I'd like to go to that new place. We're losing time. Let's set a date, we keep delaying, delaying!" They died just in time, both of them: alive to the end.

I forgot to cut a lock of their hair, and that's not like me. When my cat died, I saved a tuft of his fur. Florence was relieved: "I'm glad to see that you still distinguish between humans and animals."

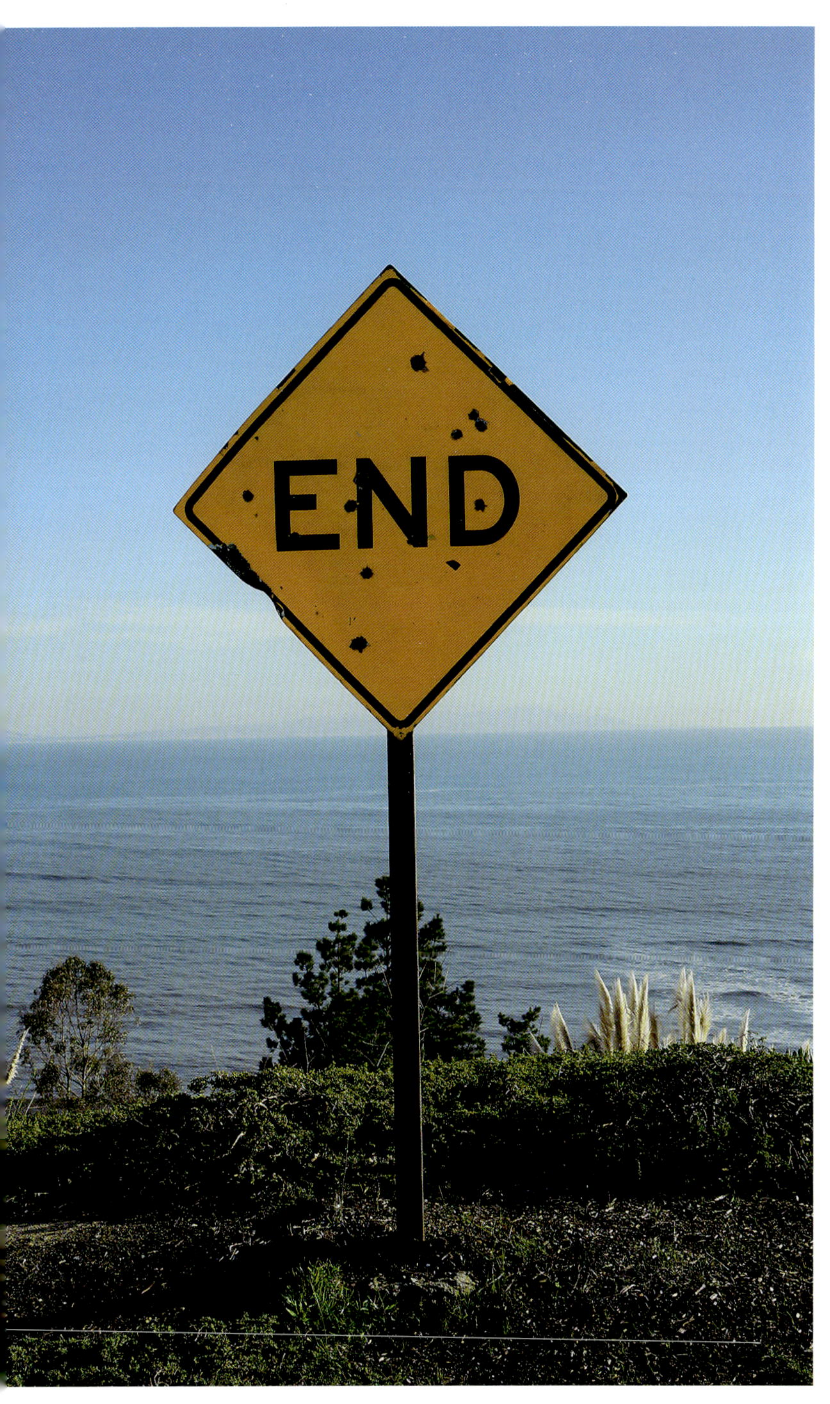
END

Parce que, au moment où mon regard vagabonde, elle entre dans la cour du restaurant où je suis attablée
Parce que, sans jamais nous regarder, elle se met à nous mitrailler avec son téléphone
Parce qu'elle a l'air de viser quelque chose au-dessus de nos têtes et qu'il n'y a rien au-dessus de nos têtes
Parce qu'elle porte une simple combinaison en nylon noir
Parce que son corps
Parce que ses jambes écartées
Parce que Goya

Because just as my attention strays, she walks into the courtyard of the restaurant where I'm seated at a table • Because without ever looking at us, she starts firing off countless shots with her phone • Because she seems to be aiming at something above our heads and there is nothing above our heads • Because she's wearing a simple black nylon slip • Because of her body • Because of her legs spread wide • Because of Goya

Mind Stories

Because, 2018...

Because

Felt curtains embroidered with text hide a series of images and explain the reasons why each picture was taken before revealing the photograph itself.

The Unknown Woman

Parce que je suis là, sur le pont
Parce que je suis avec Marie qui ne prend pas de photographies
Parce que nous sommes seules
Parce que c'est l'usage quand on est au bout du monde
Parce que je ne reviendrai pas de sitôt au pôle Nord
Parce que je ne résiste pas
Parce que le silence
Parce que la solennité
Parce que le jour alors que c'est la nuit
Parce que ce bleu, le ciel clair, la mer sombre
Parce que nous sommes un 11 septembre
Parce que je veux croire à cette image
Parce qu'on ne sait jamais
Pour le souvenir

Because I am there, on the bridge

Because I am with Marie who doesn't take pictures

Because we are alone

Because that's what you do when you are at the ends of the earth

Because I won't be back to the North Pole any time soon

Because I can't resist

Because of the silence

Because of the solemnity

Because of day when it's night

Because of the blue, the clear sky, the grey sea

Because it is the night of September 11

Because I want to believe in this image

Because you never know

For the memory of it

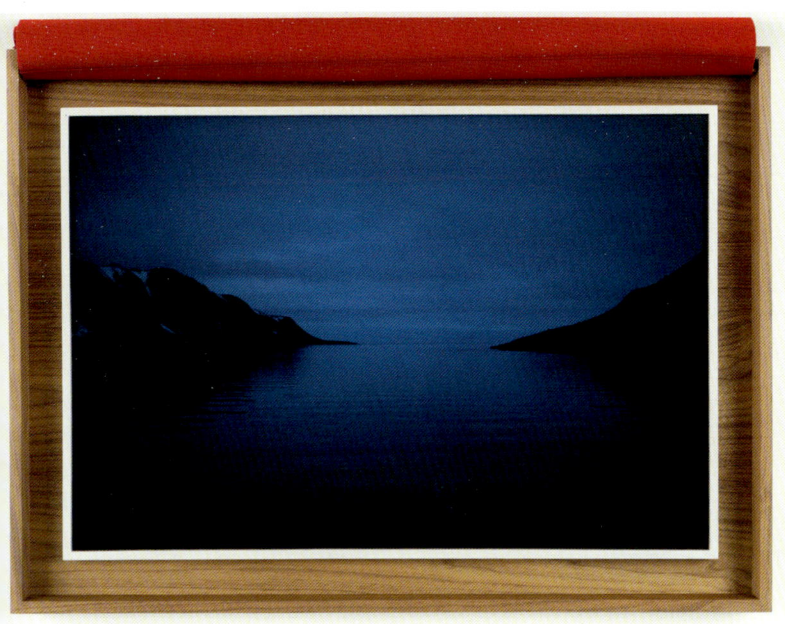

North Pole

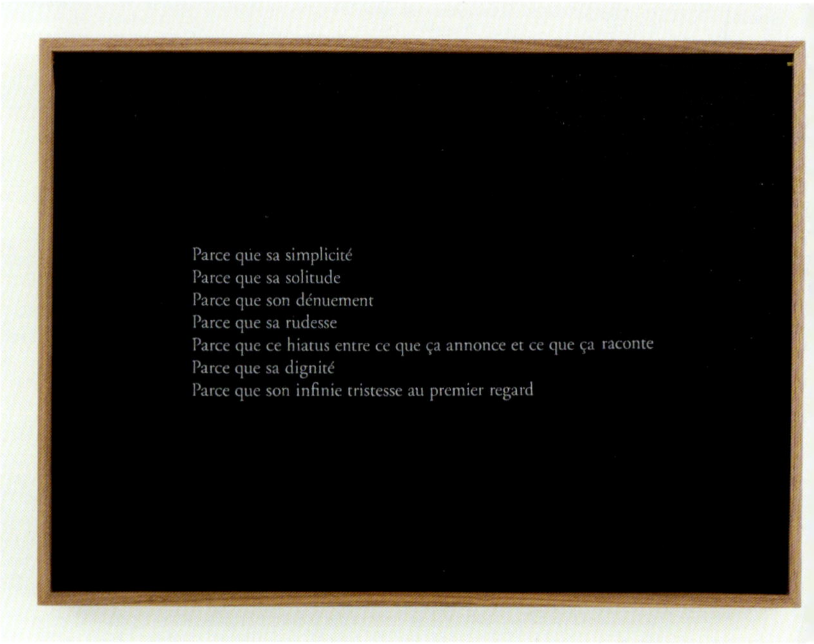

Parce que sa simplicité
Parce que sa solitude
Parce que son dénuement
Parce que sa rudesse
Parce que ce hiatus entre ce que ça annonce et ce que ça raconte
Parce que sa dignité
Parce que son infinie tristesse au premier regard

Because it is simple

Because it is lonely

Because it is bare

Because it is rough

Because of the hiatus between what it claims to be and what it is

Because of its dignity

Because of its infinite sadness

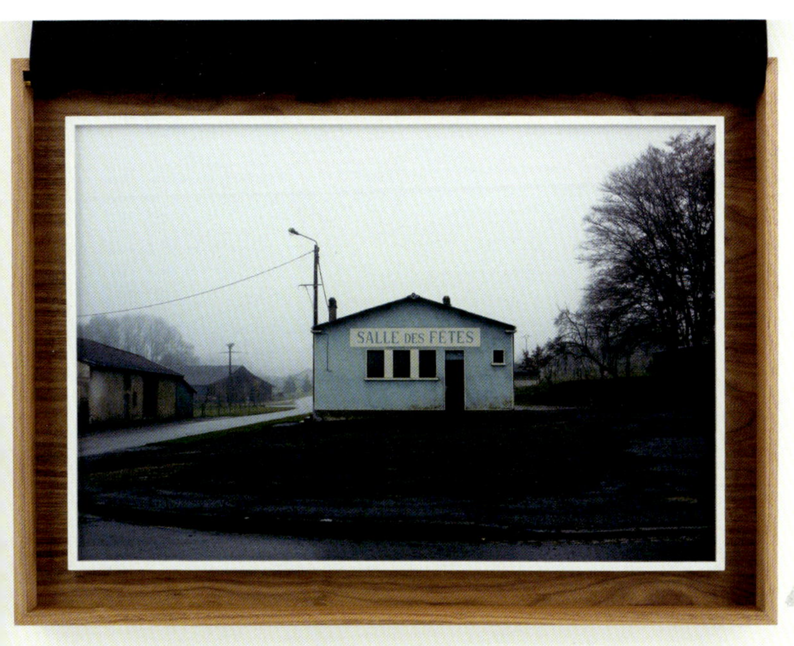

Party Hall

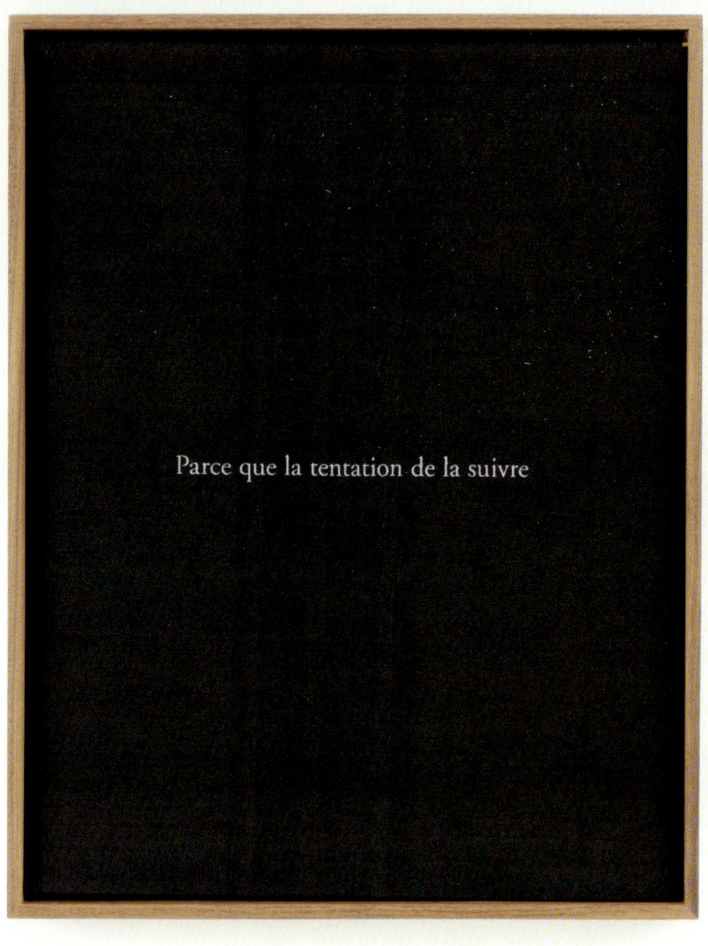

Because of the temptation to follow it

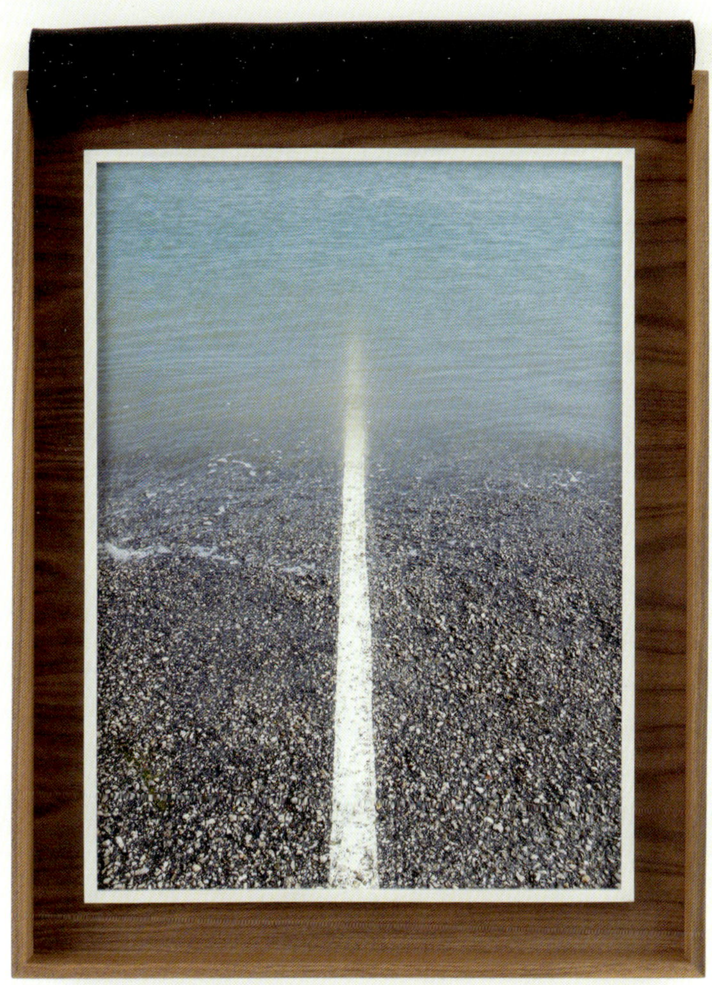

The White Line

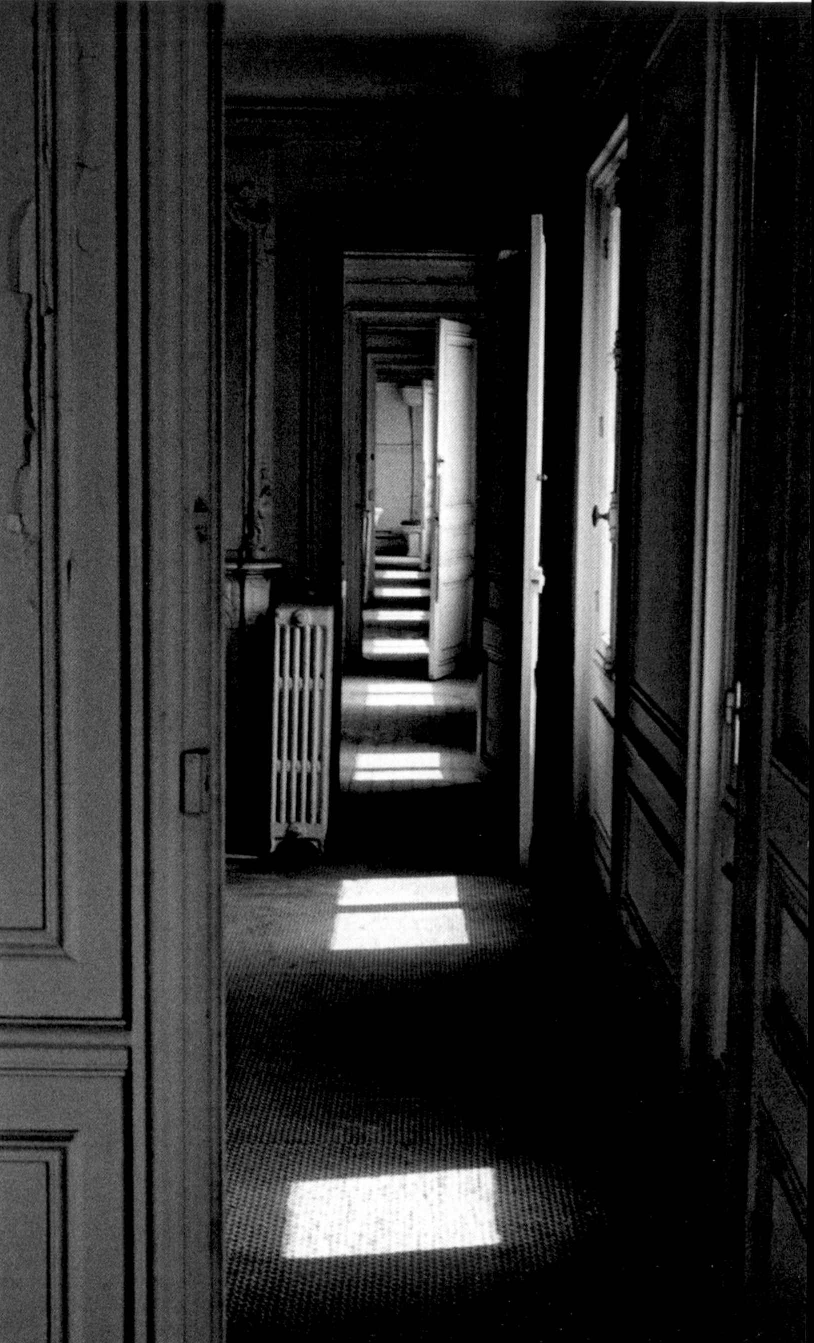

A Story Old and New

The Ghosts of Orsay, 1978–2022

1978. The last days of the year. I was back in France, in Paris, and I was walking along the quays of the Seine. At the old Gare d'Orsay, I noticed a little wooden door. Instinctively, or out of habit, I gave it a push. The door opened. A grand staircase, five stories, a ballroom, kitchens, long corridors connecting more than two-hundred and fifty rooms: the Grand Hôtel Palais d'Orsay had lain abandoned for five years. In February 1979, I went off to follow the footsteps of a stranger in Venice. Then, from April 1 to 9, I invited strangers to sleep in my bed. It wasn't until April 24 that I wrote in my diary: *Hôtel Orsay reconnect*. I went back. The door opened. I reconnected.

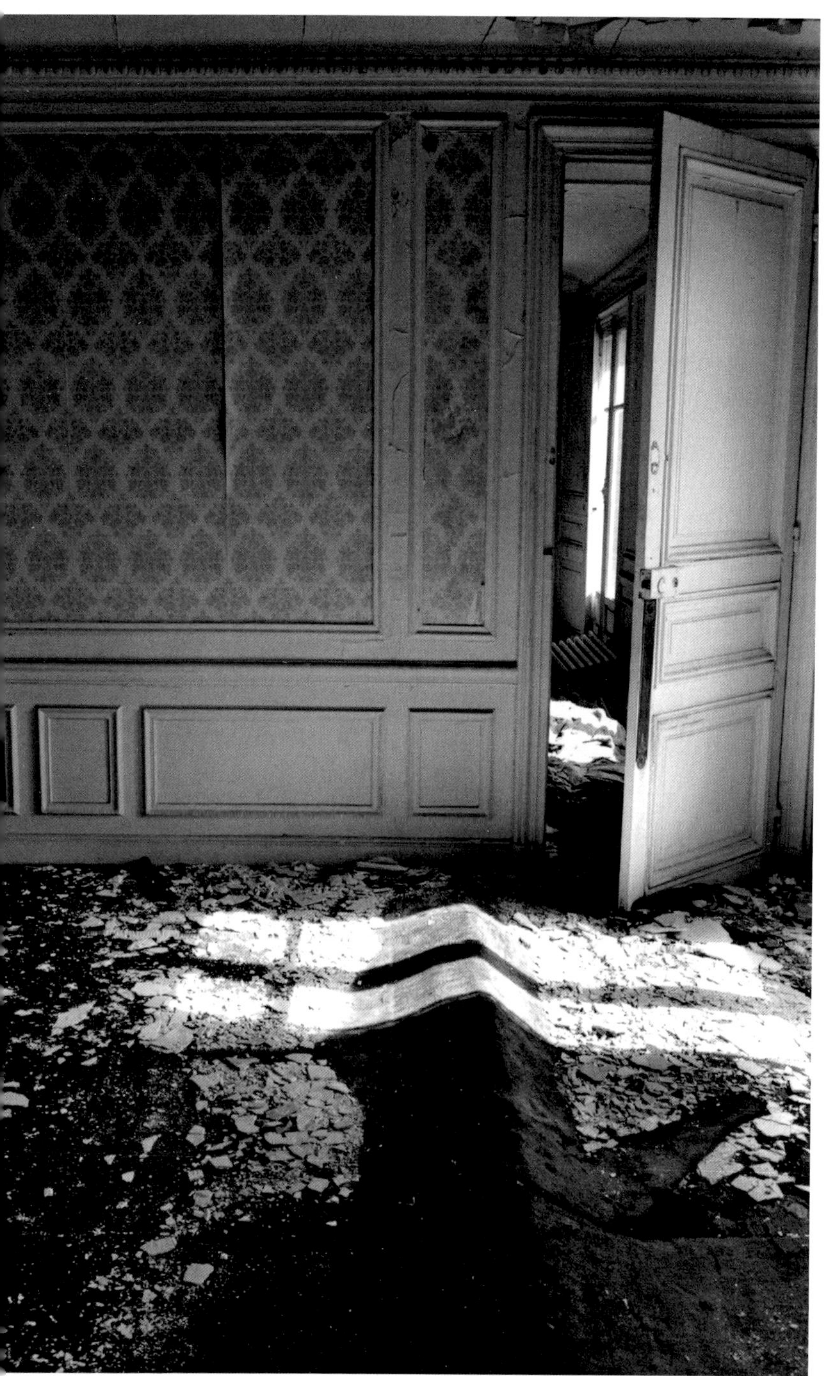

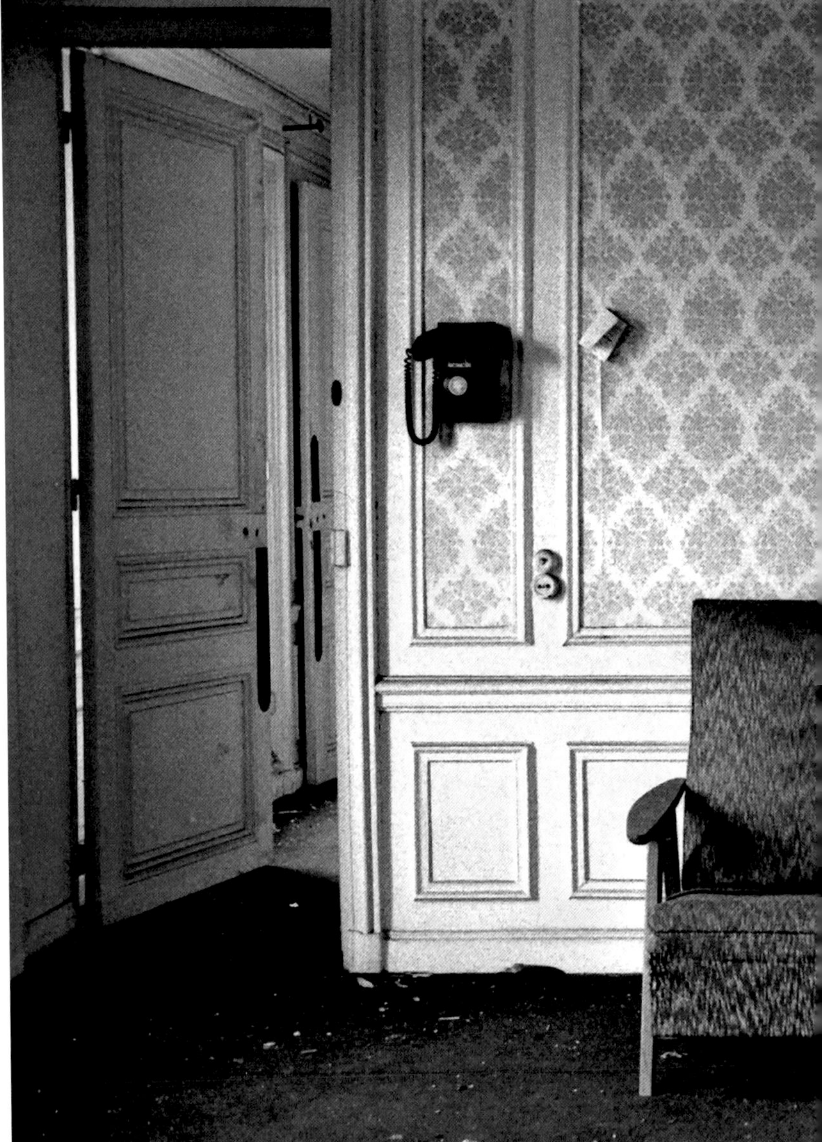

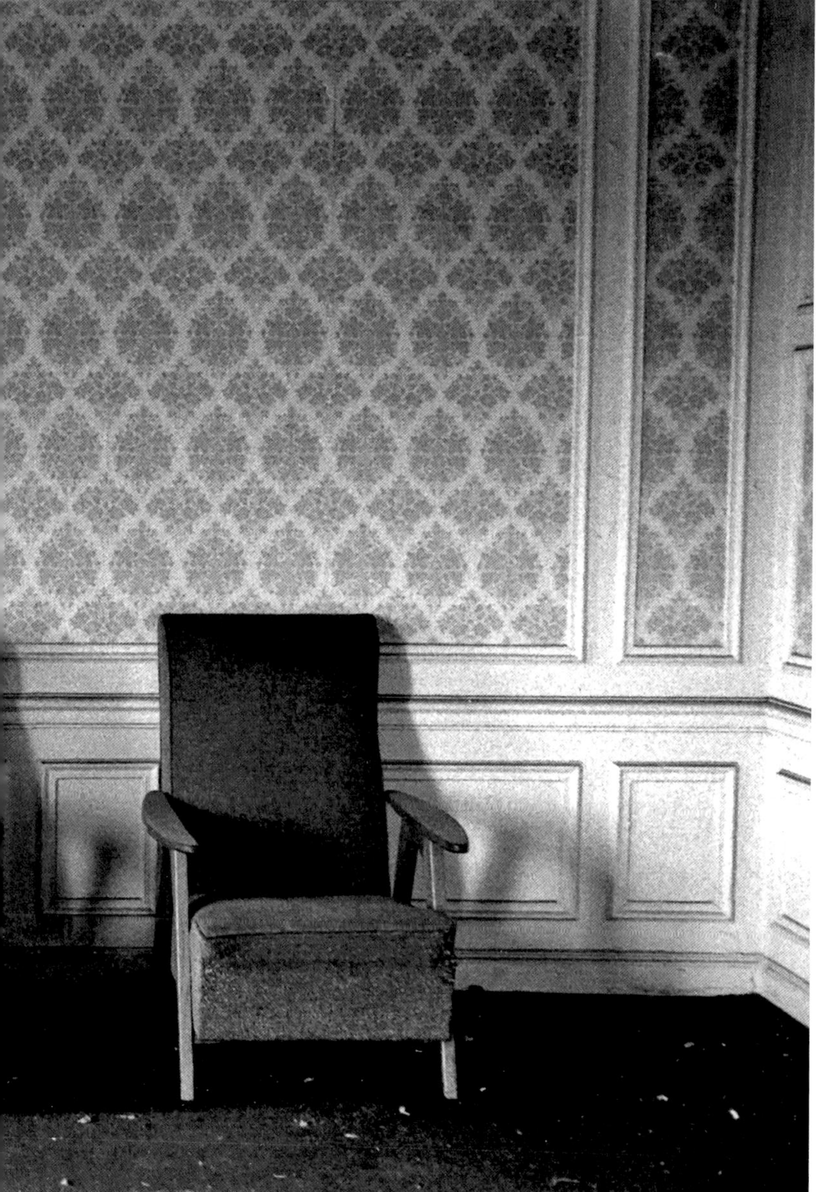

Bibliography

1983 *Suite vénitienne*, afterword by Jean Baudrillard, "Écrits sur l'image", Éditions de l'Étoile, Paris. English edition: Bay Press, Seattle, 1988.

1984 *L'Hôtel*, "Écrits sur l'image", Éditions de l'Étoile, Paris.

1989 *Le Carnet d'adresses*, facsimile edition of the original series of articles published in *Libération* in August 1983.

1991 *La Fille du docteur*, artist's book, 230 copies, Thea Westreich, New York.

1994 *Des histoires vraies*, Actes Sud, Arles; Sollertis, Toulouse.
Het adresboekje, Uitgeverij Duizend & Een, Amsterdam.
The Detachment, G+B Arts International/Arndt & Partner, Berlin.

1996 *L'Erouv de Jérusalem*, Actes Sud, Arles.
Eruv, Jerusalem Center for Visual Arts, Jerusalem.

1997 *Comme si de rien n'était*, Fondation Ledig-Rowohlt/Château de Lavigny, Vaud.

1998 *Double-jeux*, slipcase of 7 books: *De l'obéissance*, *Le Rituel d'anniversaire*, *Les Panoplies*, *À suivre...*, *L'Hôtel*, *Le Carnet d'adresses*, *Gotham Handbook*, with the participation of Paul Auster, Actes Sud, Arles.

1999 *True Stories*, Heibonsha, Tokyo.
Double Game, with the participation of Paul Auster, Violette Editions, London.

2000 *L'Absence*, slipcase of 3 books: *Souvenirs de Berlin-Est*, *Disparitions*, *Fantômes*, Actes Sud, Arles.

2001 *Les Dormeurs*, set of 2 books, Actes Sud, Arles.

2002 *Appointment*, Violette Editions, London.
Des histoires vraies, Actes Sud, Arles; *Wahre Geschichten*, Prestel, Munich; *Histórias Reais*, Agir Editora, Rio de Janeiro.
New York, Kullanma Kilavuzu, YKY, Istanbul.
The Bronx, artist's book, 250 copies, Item, Paris.
Los Angeles, artist's book, 250 copies, Item, Paris.

2003 *Douleur exquise*, Actes Sud, Arles; English edition: *Exquisite Pain*, Thames & Hudson, London
M'as-tu vue, Centre Pompidou/Éditions Xavier Barral, Paris; English edition: *Did You See Me*, Prestel, Munich.

2005 *De Eroev van Jeruzalem*, Uitgeverij Duizend & Een, Amsterdam.
Appointment with Sigmund Freud, Thames & Hudson, London.
En finir, in collaboration with Fabio Balducci, Actes Sud, Arles.

2006 *Gotham Handbook*, Maumsanchaek, Seoul.
True Stories, Maumsanchaek, Seoul.

2007 *Prenez soin de vous*/*Take Care of Yourself*, Actes Sud, Arles.

2008 *Où et quand? Berck*, with Maud Kristen, Actes Sud, Arles.

2009 *Où et quand? Berck*, *Lourdes*, *Nulle part*, with Maud Kristen, set of 3 books, Actes Sud, Arles.

2010 *True Stories*, Hasselblad Award 2010, Steidl, Göttingen.

2011 *Des histoires vraies*/*True Stories*, Actes Sud, Arles.
Aveugles/*Blind*, Actes Sud, Arles.

2012 *Moi aussi*, Éditions 591, Paris.
The Address Book, Siglio Press, Los Angeles.
Rachel, Monique..., Éditions Xavier Barral, Paris.

2013 *Souvenirs de Berlin-Est*/*Detachment*, Actes Sud, Arles.
Fantômes/*Ghosts*, Actes Sud, Arles.
Voir la mer, Actes Sud, Arles.
Des histoires vraies/*True Stories*, Actes Sud, Arles.

2014 *Exquisite Pain*, Common Master Press, Taipei, Taiwan. New ed.: Chu Chen Books, Beijing.

2015 *Suite vénitienne*, Siglio Press, Los Angeles.
Exquisite Pain, Sodam & Taeil Publishing Co., Seoul.
Tout/*My All*, Actes Sud, Arles.

2016 *Des histoires vraies*/*True Stories*/*Historias reales*, Actes Sud, Arles; La Fábrica, Madrid.
Ainsi de suite, Éditions Xavier Barral, Paris.

And so Forth, Prestel, Munich/London/
New York.

2019 *Que faites-vous de vos morts?*,
Actes Sud, Arles.

2020 *Sans lui*, Éditions Xavier Barral, Paris.

2021 *The Hotel*, Siglio Press, New York.
Wahre Geschichten, Bibliothek Suhrkamp,
Berlin.
Exquisite Pain, Chu Chen Books, Beijing.
Sophie Calle, exhibition catalogue, Centre
Pompidou Málaga, Málaga.

2022 *L'ascenseur occupe la 501/The Elevator
Resides in 501*, with Jean-Paul Demoule,
Actes Sud, Arles.
Sanna historier, Bokförlaget Faethon, Solna.
Storie vere, Contrasto, Rome.

Solo Exhibitions

1980 *The Bronx*, Fashion Moda, New York.

1981 *Les Dormeurs*, Galerie Canon, Geneva.

1983 *L'Hôtel C.*, Galerie Chantal Crousel, Paris.

1984 *L'Hôtel C.*, Galerie Formi, Nîmes.

1985 *Sophie Calle*, Apac, Centre d'Art Contemporain, Nevers.

1986 *Anatoli*, École des Beaux-Arts, Dunkirk; Centre d'Art Contemporain, Orléans.
Les Aveugles/The Blind, Galerie Crousel-Hussenot, Paris; Tasmanian College of the Arts, Hobart; De Appel, Amsterdam.

1987 *J'ai rencontré des gens qui sont nés aveugles*, Centre d'Art, Flaine, France.
Anatoli, Museotrain du Frac Limousin, Limoges, France.

1988 *Sophie Calle*, Galería Montenegro, Madrid.

1989 *Sophie Calle: A Survey*, Fred Hoffman Gallery, Los Angeles.

1990 *Sophie Calle: A Survey*, Institute of Contemporary Art, Boston.
The Sleepers, University of California, Matrix, Berkeley, CA.
Les Tombes, Galería La Máquina Española, Seville; Galerie Crousel-Robelin Bama, Paris.

1991 *Sophie Calle*, Luhring Augustine Gallery, New York; Pat Hearn Gallery, New York.
À suivre, ARC, Musée d'Art Moderne, Paris.
Sophie Calle in under skinnet, Kulturhuset, Stockholm.

1992 *The Graves*, Mills College Art Gallery, Oakland, CA.
À suivre, Lunds Konsthall, Lund, Sweden.
Sophie Calle, Donald Young Gallery, Seattle.
Pierre tombale, Centre Culturel Français, Palermo.
Les Tombes, Galerie Sollertis, Toulouse.

1993 *Blind Color*, Leo Castelli Gallery, New York.
Proofs, Hood Museum of Art, Dartmouth College, Hanover, NH.
Los Ciegos, Las Tumbas, Anatoli, Sala Mendoza, Caracas; Museo de Arte Contemporáneo, Maracay, Venezuela.

1994 *L'Absence*, Museum Boijmans Van Beuningen, Rotterdam; Galerie Chantal Crousel, Paris; Musée Cantonal des Beaux-Arts, Lausanne.
The Husband, Fraenkel Gallery, San Francisco.
The Sleepers, Bockley Gallery, Minneapolis.
Les Aveugles, Sala Amárica, Vitoria-Gasteiz.
Romances, Contemporary Arts Museum, Houston.
Des histoires vraies, Frac PACA, Marseille; Toulouse, Galerie Sollertis.

1995 *Fravaer*, Portalen, Copenhagen.
Proof, AD&A Museum, University of California, Santa Barbara, CA; Cleveland Center for Contemporary Art, Cleveland, OH; David Winton Bell Gallery, Brown University, Providence, RI.
Les Autobiographies, Printemps department store, Cahors.
Les Tombes, Galerie Arndt & Partner, Berlin.

1996 *True Stories*, Tel Aviv Museum of Art, Tel Aviv.
The Eruv of Jerusalem, Artfocus, International Biennal of Contemporary Art, Jerusalem.
Sophie Calle, High Museum of Art, Atlanta.
True Stories, Gallery Koyanagi, Tokyo.
L'Erouv, Rencontres Internationales de la Photographie, Librairie Actes Sud, Arles; Jornadas de Arte Contemporânea, Sinagoga do Porto, Porto.
The Detachment/Die Entfernung, Arndt & Partner, Berlin.
Relatos, Fundación La Caixa, Madrid.

1998 *L'Hôtel. La sphère de l'intime*, Printemps department store, Cahors.
Doubles-jeux/Double Game, Centre National de la Photographie, Paris; Site Gallery, Sheffield.
The Detachment/Die Entfernung, Kulturwissenschaftliches Institut, Essen.
The Birthday Ceremony, Tate Britain, London.
L'Erouv, Musée d'Art et d'Histoire du Judaïsme, Paris.

1999 *Les Tombes*, Galerie Clara Rainhorn, Brussels.
Doubles-jeux/Double Game, Galerie Erna Hécey, Luxembourg; Galerie Sollertis, Toulouse; Camden Arts Centre, London.

Appointment with Sigmund Freud, Freud Museum, London.
Souvenirs de Berlin-Est, Musée d'Art Moderne et Contemporain, Strasbourg.
De l'obéissance, Arndt & Partner, Berlin.
Double Game, Gallery Koyanagi, Tokyo.
Exquisite Pain, Hara Museum of Contemporary Art, Tokyo.
The Eruv, Jewish Museum, New York.

2000 *Die wahren Geschichten der Sophie Calle*, Fridericianum, Kassel; Staatliche Kunsthalle, Baden-Baden.
Sophie Calle..., Librairie des Archives, Paris.
Sophie Calle, École Régionale des Beaux-Arts, Dunkirk.
Souvenirs de Berlin-Est, Rencontres Internationales de la Photographie, Librairie Actes Sud, Arles.
Sophie Calle – Sol LeWitt, Donald Young Gallery, Chicago.

2001 *Double Game*, Paula Cooper Gallery, New York.
Sophie Calle, Public Places – Private Spaces, Contemporary Jewish Museum, San Francisco.
Vingt ans après, Galerie Perrotin, Paris.
Éditions, Galerie Perrotin, Paris.

2002 *Gotham Handbook*, Arndt & Partner, Berlin.
Sophie Calle, Spectrum, International Prize for Photography of the Foundation of Lower Saxony, Sprengel Museum, Hanovre.

2003 *M'as-tu vue*, Centre Pompidou, Paris.
Dommages collatéraux, Galerie Perrotin, Paris.
Sophie Calle, Toyota Municipal Museum of Art, Toyota.
Editions, Gallery Koyanagi, Tokyo.

2004 *M'as-tu vue*, Irish Museum of Modern Art, Dublin; Ludwig Forum, Aix-la-Chapelle; Martin-Gropius-Bau, Berlin.
True Stories, Arndt & Partner, Berlin.
Die Entfernung – The Detachment, Kunst im Deutschen Bundestag, Berlin.

2005 *Exquisite Pain*, Paula Cooper Gallery, New York; Art Museum, Portland.

2006 *Le Téléphone*, in collaboration with Frank Gehry, Pont du Garigliano, Paris.
True Stories, Galerie Perrotin, Miami.

2007 *Prenez soin de vous*, French Pavilion at the 52nd Venice Biennale.

Exquisite Pain (staging by Frank Gehry & Edwin Chan), Rotunda 1, Bonnevoie, Luxembourg.

2008 *Où et quand? Berck, Lourdes*, Galerie Perrotin, Paris.
Prenez soin de vous, Fondation pour l'Art Contemporain DHC/ART, Montreal; BNF, Richelieu site, Paris.

2009 *The Address Book*, Gemini GEL, Los Angeles.
Talking to Strangers, Whitechapel Gallery, London.
Cuide de você, Museu de Arte Moderna, Rio de Janeiro; Museu de Arte Moderna da Bahia, Salvador; SESC Pompeia, São Paulo.
calle sophie, Palais des Beaux-Arts, Brussels.
No Sex Last Night, Oi Futuro Flamengo, Rio de Janeiro.
Take Care of Yourself, Paula Cooper Gallery, New York.
Où et quand? Berck, Lourdes, Arndt & Partner, Berlin.

2010 *Sophie Calle: 2010 Hasselblad Award Winner*, Hasselblad Foundation, Gothenburg.
Rachel, Monique..., Friche du Palais de Tokyo, Paris.
Where and When? Lourdes, Art Gallery Christina Wilson, Copenhagen.
Talking to Strangers, Louisiana Museum of Modern Art, Humlebaek, Denmark; De Pont Museum, Tilburg, Netherlands.

2011 *Take Care of Yourself/Hoia end. Ole tubli*, Tallinna Kunstihoone, Tallinn.
Son Kez, Ilk Kez, Sakıp Sabancı Müzesi, Istanbul.
True Stories, Prospect.2, 1850 House of the Louisiana State Museum, New Orleans.
Room, Crossing the Line Festival, Lowell Hotel, New York.

2012 *Pour la dernière et pour la première fois*, Galerie Perrotin, Paris.
Pour la dernière et pour la première fois, Rencontres d'Arles, Chapelle du Méjan, Arles.
Rachel, Monique..., Festival d'Avignon, Église des Célestins, Avignon.
Historias de pared, Banco de la República, Bogotá.
Moi aussi, Musée du Septennat, Château-Chinon.

Historias de pared, Museo de Arte Moderno de Medellín, Medellín.
Take Care of Yourself, Espoo Museum of Modern Art, Espoo, Finland; Pulitzer Arts Foundation, Saint Louis, MO.
2013 *Dérobés*, Galerie Perrotin, Paris.
Last Seen, Isabella Stewart Gardner Museum, Boston.
Absence, Paula Cooper Gallery, New York.
Chambre 20, Hôtel La Mirande, Avignon.
Où et quand?, 313 Art Project, Seoul.
For the Last and First Time, Hara Museum of Contemporary Art, Tokyo.
Take Care of Yourself, Lillehammer Kunstmuseum, Lillehammer, Norway; Stavanger Kunstmuseum, Stavanger, Norway.
2014 *Sophie Calle, Makoto Aida*, Galerie Perrotin, Hong Kong.
Cuídese mucho, Museo Tamayo, Mexico City.
MAdRE, Castello di Rivoli, Turin.
Sophie Calle: An Introduction, Un Cabinet d'Amateur, Sofia, Bulgaria.
Cuídese mucho, Museo de Arte Contemporáneo, Monterrey, Mexico.
Rachel, Monique…, Church of the Heavenly Rest, New York.
Voir la mer, Church of Notre-Dame de l'Assomption, Valloire, France.
2015 *Sophie Calle*, Fraenkel Gallery, San Francisco.
For the Last and First Time, Toyota Municipal Museum of Art, Toyota.
Cuídese mucho, Centro Cultural Kirchner, Buenos Aires.
Modus vivendi, La Virreina Centre de la Imatge, Barcelona.
Sophie Calle: North Pole, University of Michigan Museum of Art, Ann Arbor, MI.
Pour la dernière et pour la première fois, Musée d'Art Contemporain, Montreal.
2016 *Histoires vraies*, Théâtre Liberté, Toulon, France.
For the Last and First Time, Nagasaki Prefectural Art Museum, Nagasaki.
A View of my Life, Arndt & Partner, Berlin.
2017 *Midnight Moment: Voir la mer*, Crossing the Line Festival, Institut Français, New York.
Beau doublé monsieur le marquis!, Musée de la Chasse et de la Nature, Paris.
Histoires vraies, Théâtre Vidy-Lausanne, Lausanne, Switzerland.
Missing, Fort Mason Center, San Francisco.
My Mother, my Cat, my Father, in that Order, Fraenkel Lab, San Francisco.
2018 *Dead End,* Château La Coste, Aix-en-Provence.
L'Hôtel / Voir la mer, Espace Louis Vuitton, Munich.
Parce que & Souris Calle, Galerie Perrotin, Paris.
2019 *Regard Incertain*, Kunstmuseum Thun, Thun, Switzerland.
Un certain regard, Fotomuseum, Winterthur, Switzerland.
Ma mère, mon chat, mon père, dans cet ordre, Galerie Perrotin, Tokyo.
Because, Gallery Koyanagi, Tokyo.
Voir la mer, Shibuya Crossing, Tokyo.
Exquisite Pain, Hara Museum of Contemporary Art, Tokyo.
Cinq (Histoires vraies / Voir la mer / Rachel, Monique… / Parce que / Liberté surveillée, À l'espère, Le Chasseur français), Musée Grobet-Labadié / Château Borély / Chapelle du Centre de la Vieille-Charité / Musée des Beaux-Arts / Muséum d'Histoire Naturelle, Marseille.
Cuídese mucho, Museo de Arte Contemporáneo, Santiago de Chile.
2020 *Because*, Fraenkel Gallery, San Francisco.
Les Aveugles / Was Bleibt, Kunstmuseum Ravensburg, Germany.
2021 *Sophie Calle*, Centre Pompidou Málaga, Málaga.
2022 *Les fantômes d'Orsay*, Musée d'Orsay, Paris.

Group Exhibitions

1980 11e Biennale des Jeunes, ARC, Musée d'Art Moderne, Paris.
Une idée en l'air, The Clocktower and Fashion Moda, New York.

1981 *Autoportraits*, Centre Pompidou, Paris.

1983 *À Pierre & Marie*, 36, rue d'Ulm, Paris.

1989 *Histoires de musée*, Musée d'Art Moderne, Paris.

1990 Sydney Biennale, Sydney.
Seven Obsessions, Whitechapel Gallery, London.
Images in Transition: Photographic Representation Towards the 90's, National Museum of Modern Art, Kyoto; National Museum of Modern Art, Tokyo.

1991 *Dislocations*, Museum of Modern Art, New York; Carnegie International, Pittsburgh, PA.

1992 *Doubletake: Collective Memory and Contemporary Art*, Hayward Gallery, London.

1993 *Whitney Biennial*, Whitney Museum of American Art, New York.
Blind Color, Leo Castelli, New York.

1994 *Some Went Mad... Some Ran Away*, Serpentine Gallery, London; Museum of Contemporary Art, Chicago; Portalen, Copenhagen.
Beyond Photography, Israel Museum, Jerusalem; Ludwig Museum, Cologne; Serpentine Gallery, London; Boca Raton Museum of Art, Boca Raton, FL; Contemporary Arts Museum, Houston; High Museum of Art, Atlanta; Philadelphia Museum of Art, Philadelphia; Museum of Photographic Art, San Diego; Museum of Contemporary Art, Chicago.

1995 *Féminin/masculin. Le sexe de l'art*, Centre Pompidou, Paris.

1996 *NowHere*, Louisiana Museum of Modern Art, Humlebaek, Denmark.
L'Expérience du monochrome..., Musée d'Art Contemporain, Lyon.

1997 *Trade Routes: History and Geography*, Johannesburg Biennale, Johannesburg.

1998 *Deep Storage – Arsenale der Erinnerung*, Kunstmuseum Düsseldorf, Düsseldorf.
Premises, Guggenheim Museum, New York.
La Sphère de l'intime, Printemps department store, Cahors.

1999 *Museum as Muse*, Museum of Modern Art, New York.

2002 *Stories*, Haus der Kunst, Munich.

2003 *Warum!*, Martin-Gropius-Bau, Berlin.

2011 *For the Last and First Time*, 12th Istanbul Biennial, Sakip Sabanci Museum, Istanbul.

2012 *Spies in the House of Art*, Metropolitan Museum of Art, New York.
Sophie Calle, Christian Marclay, Paul Pfeiffer, Walid Raad, Michael Sailstorfer, Carey Young, Paula Cooper Gallery, New York.

2014 *S'il y a lieu je pars avec vous*, Le Bal, Paris.
Unsold, Gallery Koyanagi, Tokyo.

2017 *Deutsche Börse Photography Foundation Prize Shortlist*, The Photographers' Gallery, London; Museum für moderne Kunst, Frankfurt.

2020 *Push the Limits*, Fondazione Merz, Turin.
Le Supermarché des images, Jeu de Paume, Paris.

2021 *Mother!*, Louisiana Museum of Modern Art, Humlebaek, Denmark; Kunsthalle Mannheim, Mannheim.
Le supermarché des images, Red Brick Art Museum, Beijing.

2022 *Women and Change*, Arken Museum of Modern Art, Ishøj, Denmark.
Spectra: A Century in Color, Bundeskunsthalle, Bonn.

Text credits

Extracts from *The Sleepers*, *Twenty Years
    Later*, *Because*:
Courtesy of Editions Xavier Barral, Paris

Extracts from *The Hotel*, *The Shadow*,
    Suite vénitienne:
From Sophie Calle: *Double Game*, 1999 & 2007
Courtesy of Violette Editions

Suite vénitienne was translated from the
    French by Dany Barash and Danny Hatfield
    and first published in English in 1988 by
    Bay Press, Seattle.

Extract from *On the Hunt*:
First published in English in *Wallpaper**
    magazine, November 2020

Extracts from:
    The Elevator Resides in 501:
    Peter Behrman de Sinéty
    True Stories: Anthony Allen
    and Hanford Woods
    The Blind: Charles Penwarden
    Take Care of Yourself: Charles Penwarden
    (+ Cole Swensen/Sandra Reid/John Tittensor)
    Ghosts: Charles Penwarden
Courtesy of Actes Sud, Arles

All efforts have been made to trace the owners
of the copyright for all of the texts that appear
in this book. Thames & Hudson will be happy
to rectify any omissions or errors in future
printings of this book.

The Photofile series is the original English-language
edition of the Photo Poche collection. It was first
published between 1986 and 1992 by the Centre
National de la Photographie, Paris, with the support
of the French Ministry of Culture. Robert Delpire
(1926–2017) was the creator of the series and its
managing editor until 2017.

Picture credits
Pages 14, 18, 19, 25, 47: Jean-Baptiste Mondino
Page 27: Yves Roujon
Page 69: Richard Baltauss
Pages 131, 133: The Hunting Federations of Loir-et-Cher and Loiret
(CCTV images taken on the A85 and A19 autoroutes)

General editor: Géraldine Lay

Series design by Matthew Young

Introduction translated from the French by Ruth Taylor

First published in the United Kingdom in 2022 by
Thames & Hudson Ltd, 181A High Holborn, London WC1V 7QX

First published in the United States of America in 2022 by
Thames & Hudson Inc., 500 Fifth Avenue, New York, New York 10110

British Library Cataloguing-in-Publication Data
A catalogue record for this book is available from the British Library

Library of Congress Control Number 2022938433

ISBN 978-0-500-41121-6
Printed and bound in Italy

Be the first to know about our new releases,
exclusive content and author events by visiting
thamesandhudson.com
thamesandhudsonusa.com
thamesandhudson.com.au